CHI KUNG
FOR HEALTH
AND
VITALITY

A PRACTICAL APPROACH
TO THE ART OF ENERGY

By the same author

The Art of Chi Kung
The Complete Book of Tai Chi Chuan
The Complete Book of Zen
The Art of Shaolin Kung Fu

To obtain a copy, simply telephone TBS Direct on 01206 255800

For Mr. Wong's web site, please visit
www.geocities.com/~wahnam

CONTENTS

LIST OF ILLUSTRATIONS

This book is dedicated to the fond memory of
my late father, Wong York Sang,
who, although he had never practised chi kung,
still lived to a ripe old age,
mainly because he had a loving heart

PREFACE

Would you like to have good health and vitality, freshness of mind and inner peace? This book will show you how to accomplish these aims by practising chi kung.

Chi kung is both an ancient art and modern science. It refers to the training and application of cosmic energy for our various needs, particularly for health, internal force, mental development and spiritual growth, which can be used by anyone, irrespective of race, culture or religion. Arts of energy were practised esoterically by various peoples of the great ancient civilizations, and were known by different names, such as yoga, the art of mysteries and the art of wisdom, by the Indians, Egyptians and Tibetans respectively. The Chinese call these previously arcane arts 'chi kung'.

In the past knowledge of chi kung was a jealously guarded secret, taught only to selected disciples. But conditions have changed, and chi kung masters now sincerely wish to spread a knowledge and understanding of chi kung for the good of all humanity. Indeed, chi kung has much to offer to today's world, as I will explain in this book.

There is at present an urgent need for reliable information about chi kung, especially for English readers. The few books in English about chi kung are mainly descriptions of chi kung with little philosophical background. Others, which have largely been translated literally from Chinese texts, can be hard to follow as technical terms are not explained in a vocabulary and imagery that English readers can understand. This book, and its earlier companion *The Art of Chi Kung*, which is also published by Element, attempt to overcome these two problems. I would like to take this opportunity to thank the many readers who have kindly taken the trouble to write to me to express their appreciation of the earlier book; some of them invited me to their countries to teach chi kung, and some asked me to continue writing. This book, *Chi Kung for Health and Vitality*, is the answer to their earnest requests.

Although these two books are related, they are independent of each other. While the first book is a comprehensive, philosophical introduction to the wonders of chi kung, this second book is a practical guide. Of the various dimensions of chi kung, those of health and vitality are emphasized in this book, though the other dimensions are also mentioned. Chi kung is a preventive-cum-curative system par excellence. Those who have long suffered from so-called incurable diseases such as hypertension, asthma, ulcers, rheumatic pains, diabetes, insomnia and depression can hope for a possible cure if they practise the chi kung exercises described in this book, just as thousands of chi kung practitioners have been cured in chi kung classes conducted by me or my disciples. As well as describing the methods which have relieved innumerable people of their chronic or degenerative diseases, this book also includes explanations of how chi kung works.

More important than curing diseases, chi kung prevents illness, increases vitality and promotes longevity. This book discusses both the principles and the practices that are effective in achieving these aims. So, if you read this book and are still not healthy and full of vitality, it is not for want of knowledge, but lack of training.

From the chi kung perspective, health includes not only physical, but also emotional, mental and spiritual well-being. The book explains how and why chi kung can help you to achieve emotional maturity, mental freshness and spiritual growth, irrespective of your religion or beliefs.

All the chi kung exercises described in this book are selected from methods actually practised and found effective in my many chi kung classes. Numerous case histories are also provided for inspiration. The historical examples are taken from authoritative chi kung literature, and all the recent case histories described are true cases. These are usually taken from my own teaching experience, but the names of the persons involved have been changed for ethical and other reasons.

Some of the accomplishments of the chi kung practitioners mentioned in this book may appear incredible to some readers. However, all these attainments are verifiable; they are abilities or experiences that I have witnessed personally. Readers of this book may often exclaim that facts are indeed stranger than fiction. But by the time they have read much of the book, and become more familiar with the principles and practice of chi kung, they may perhaps conclude that these strange facts are logical and natural after all.

Wong Kiew Kit
Grandmaster
Shaolin Wahnam Chi Kung Institute

1

TREAT YOURSELF TO THE SECRETS OF THE ANCIENT MASTERS

An Introduction to Chi Kung

❖ *A person may have spent many years practising chi kung, yet he may not have gone into it deeply because he lacks the philosophical background and the once secretly guarded methodology.*

Chi Kung or Qigong?

Would you like to have health and vitality? One of the best ways to realize this aim, proven throughout the ages, is to practise chi kung. And this book will show you how.

By now many people have heard of chi kung, but many more people, even among the Chinese, do not know what chi kung really is; even fewer people are aware that when they practise genuine chi kung – not some adulterated exercises pretending to its name – they are practising some of the secrets of ancient masters.

Cki Kung is spelt 'qigong' in Romanized Chinese. If we think that Romanized Chinese is unphonetic, we are mistaken. Actually, 'qigong' is phonetically more exact than 'chi kung', but these Romanized spellings may sound funny to us because we are not familiar with them.

This also illustrates the simple fact that what appears familiar to us, what we often take for granted as truth, may not necessarily be the truth. I mention this fact because what you are going to read about chi kung may not necessarily agree with what you previously considered it to be.

The Four Dimensions of Chi Kung

'Chi' means energy. Some Chinese in our modern world may tell you that chi means air, which is not correct. If you look at the history of the word, it has always meant energy, long before air was understood by scientists. 'Kung' means art. So chi kung is the art of energy. In particular, chi kung refers to the art of developing life energy for health, internal power, mind cultivation and spiritual fulfilment.

Not many people, not even some chi kung practitioners, regard chi kung in this comprehensive way. My own experience can serve as a good illustration.

In the 1950s, when I was first exposed to chi kung, I imagined it to be some form of advanced martial art. At that time, very few people had heard about chi kung and most of them regarded it as an esoteric art that could enable the practitioner to injure his opponent without leaving any external marks, or to take blows and kicks from his enemy without sustaining any injury himself. We were quite right in our limited way to regard chi kung as internal kungfu as it actually constitutes one dimension of chi kung.

In China, chi kung started to become popular among the public in the 1960s, after the great master Liu Gui Zhen extensively and successfully employed chi kung therapy to treat a wide range of degenerative diseases. By 1980 it had spread to Chinese communities overseas, especially in Hong Kong, Singapore and Malaysia, where a form of chi kung called Waitankung, which literally means the 'art of external elixir' was introduced from Taiwan and was widely practised. A few years later another type of chi kung known as Taiji Eighteen Steps, which was introduced from mainland China, became very popular. These two types of chi kung, which have contributed greatly to the spread of chi kung, are principally concerned with health, and have almost nothing to do with martial arts. Thus, many people imagine that chi kung is only concerned with health, although this is just one of the dimensions of chi kung. Indeed, a few kungfu masters even went to the extent of publicly declaring that chi kung had nothing to do with martial arts!

It was at about this time that I made some very controversial statements. I said that chi kung, as well as being an excellent art for health and kungfu, can also be used to develop our minds to such a fine level that supernormal abilities are possible. This is another dimension of chi kung, the mind dimension. These statements were made to support some fantastic claims made by some of the greatest chi kung masters in China – claims of telepathy, clairvoyance, psychokinesis, and distant chi transmission. I knew that I would be attacked, but as a Shaolin disciple and chi kung grandmaster, I felt I should have the courage to tell the truth, even if most people would find it hard to accept. I also hoped that my statements might encourage other chi kung masters to work together to enhance this mind dimension, so as to bring the art to greater heights for the benefit of humanity.

Through chi kung I had cultivated my mind to a level where I could transmit chi or energy over great distance to cure illness and relieve suffering. Knowing that almost no one would believe me, I offered to allow myself to be tested publicly. I also promised publicly that I was willing to share this knowledge with other chi kung masters so that we could develop distant healing to serve humanity. These statements were widely published in local and national newspapers in my country Malaysia.

Understandably, I was severely criticized. Some people thought that I had gone mad. Nevertheless, in a series of public experiments in 1989, conducted by the independent Chinese national newspaper, the *Shin Min Daily News*, I was able to demonstrate that distant chi transmission is a reality.

I was prudent enough not to mention openly the fourth dimension of chi kung, the spiritual dimension, but only to discuss it privately with my students. I have often told my advanced students that the supreme achievement of chi kung is spiritual fulfilment – irrespective of one's religion, or even one's lack of a formal religion. Chi kung is absolutely non-religious but, at the advanced level, it is spiritual – it transcends the physical self.

But if you find the mental and the spiritual dimensions of chi kung too far-fetched to believe, then please ignore them – at least for the time being. This book is mainly about chi kung at the physical level; it is principally a practical guide to explain some useful chi kung exercises that can improve your health and vitality.

From my many years of teaching chi kung to more than 2,000

students from various walks of life, I have learnt that most people come to chi kung for health reasons – to relieve some chronic or degenerative illness, or to manage stress. Some come to increase their energy level, and for freshness of mind – to improve their sports or martial arts performance, or to enhance creativity and inspiration. Most of them are perfectly happy to experience chi kung at the physical level, and some at the mental level, leaving the spiritual dimension to the very few who have the endurance to soar to the greatest heights.

Nevertheless, though this book is intended to be a practical guide to health and vitality, it is beneficial to have, right from the start, a comprehensive view of chi kung with its four dimensions of health, martial arts, mind cultivation and spiritual development. In this way, we can avoid being 'lop-sided' in our understanding of chi kung; and even if we choose to emphasize only one particular dimension, at least we will also be aware that other dimensions are available. The following brief look at the historical background of chi kung will help give you an understanding of how these four dimensions came about.

A Brief History of Chi Kung

Chi kung was not invented by any person or persons; it is the result of a few thousand years of man's experience in and development of the use of cosmic energy for various definite purposes. Past masters developed the arts of energy for curing illness, promoting health and longevity, enhancing fighting skills, expanding the mind, attaining different levels of consciousness, and achieving spirituality. These arts of using cosmic energy developed separately, though they often influenced one another, and were known by different names, such as the Art of Developing Elixir, the Art of Internal Strengthening, and the Art of Longevity. But they all had one common factor – they all involved chi, or energy. It is only in modern times, since the 1950s, that these arts have been collectively known as chi kung, that is the 'art of energy'. For convenience, we classify these various types or arts of chi kung into five major schools, namely the medical, the martial, the Confucianist, the Taoist, and the Buddhist.

Chi kung began when prehistoric men discovered that they

could manipulate their breath, which is a form of energy, in different ways for particular purposes. For example, they found that by softly blowing 'shss…' onto a wound, they could reduce its pain; and by explosively uttering 'heit', they could marshal more strength – perhaps to lift or move heavy objects. Such knowledge was initially acquired mainly through trial and error, but gradually accumulated to form a larger body of knowledge.

Chinese records show that by 2,700 BCE, chi kung had become an important aspect of Chinese medicine. The earliest type of chi kung was probably a form of meditative dance which encouraged energy balance in the body. There were also numerous dynamic chi kung patterns devised to cure as well as prevent illness. This manifested the health dimension; and the various practices constituted what is now collectively called the medical school of chi kung.

Since the Zhou Dynasty in the 6th century BCE, Taoist hermits, whose pre-occupation was longevity, have made a great contribution to the health dimension of chi kung. However, the types of chi kung they developed were concerned not so much with the curing of diseases, as with the prevention of illness and the promotion of long life. Their principal aim was spiritual development, in attaining unity with the cosmos; and chi kung was the royal path. Their chi kung practices are collectively termed the Taoist school of chi kung. Taoist chi kung is noted for some profound breathing techniques and visualization exercises, and advanced practitioners often possess supernormal abilities.

Later, when Buddhism spread to China during the Han Dynasty (3rd century CE), Buddhist meditation greatly influenced and enriched the principles and practices of chi kung. In Buddhism, meditation is the essential way to enlightenment. Those chi kung types that are of the Buddhist tradition are now classified as the Buddhist school, and their emphasis is on mind cultivation and spiritual development. Though many Buddhist masters regarded extraordinary powers as a distraction from spiritual development, advanced chi kung practitioners of the Buddhist school often have supernormal abilities.

Chinese martial arts, especially Shaolin Kungfu, developed to a very high level during the Tang Dynasty (7th century CE). Many kungfu masters made use of chi kung to enhance their fighting abilities. These chi kung types are therefore called the martial school of chi kung. In the 13th century Taijiquan (Tai Chi Chuan), and later in the 17th century Bagua (Pakua) and Xingyi (Hsing Yi) Kungfu became popular. These 'inner styles' of Chinese martial arts emphasize the development of chi in their training.

Neo-Confucianism flourished since the Song Dynasty (10th century CE) until recent times. Many scholars, artists, scientists, philosophers and other great men of culture and learning practised and developed chi kung for freshness of mind and clarity of thought. Their chi kung types are commonly referred to as the Confucianist school. You will be surprised how far ahead of our modern scientists these classical masters were. One of the greatest philosophers, Zhang Dai, who lived in the 11th century, expounded that the universe is a body of chi (or energy): when chi integrates it forms matter which manifests as myriad things; when matter disintegrates it returns to its nebulous state of chi. Zhang Dai also mentioned that chi and matter are constantly and endlessly acting and interacting with one another.

It must be stressed that terms like Confucianist, Taoist and Buddhist, as used here and elsewhere in this book, are philosophical – not religious – in meaning. We call a certain chi kung type Confucianist, for instance, because it was, on the whole, developed and initially practised by people who followed the Confucian philosophy; just as we call the language you are reading now, English, because it was initially developed and used by people who were English. Similarly, just as you (who may or may not be English) and I (a Malaysian Chinese) can use English freely, those who may or may not be Confucianists (or Taoist or Buddhist, for that matter) can practise and benefit from Confucianist, Taoist or Buddhist chi kung without the slightest uneasiness about any religious aspects.

The Scientific Basis of Chi

Some people are tempted to say, 'Where is chi? I can't see it or feel it'. These people forget that they can't see or feel air either. Actually, chi is everywhere around us, and everywhere inside us. We normally cannot see or feel it because of the limitation of our eyes and other senses. Our eyes, for example, can only see electromagnetic waves between wavelengths of 0.4 and 0.8

micron, that is, 0.0004 and 0.0008 millimetres, whereas the known electromagnetic spectrum spans from 0.000000047 micron to over 30 kilometres! Chi happens to fall outside the exceedingly narrow range of electromagnetic waves visible to our human eyes.

Because chi is invisible to most people – although some gifted people and practitioners with supernormal abilities can actually see chi – many people think that chi is imaginary, not real. In 1977 scientists in China demonstrated that chi is real. They invited chi kung masters to channel chi from their hands to modern scientific instruments. The instruments conclusively showed that the chi of these masters consists of electromagnetic waves, infra-red rays, static energy and certain particle flows.[1]

Numerous experiments and research also confirmed that the traditional claims made by chi kung masters are valid. For example, a lay person breathes about 18 times a minute, but a chi kung practitioner breathes only about five times.[2] His breathing is not only slower and deeper, it also involves a better exchange of oxygen and carbon dioxide. In other words, a chi kung practitioner has a more efficient system for removing toxins from his body. Research has also shown that a person's breathing rate is closely related to his emotional state: the slower and deeper the breathing, the calmer a person is.

An average person takes in about 500cc of air in one breath. Through the practice of good breathing which gradually enlarges the intake capacity of the lungs, a chi kung master can take in 5,000 to 7,000cc in one breath![3] This increased supply of oxygen per breath means that a chi kung master has a greater supply of energy, which gives his body better resistance, a greater capability for self-regeneration and a more effective immune system.

Researchers found that in a 1 cm square area of the skin of a lay person, there are about 2,000 capillaries, of which only about five are normally filled with flowing blood. In the same area of the skin of a chi kung practitioner, as many as 200 capillaries are normally filled with flowing blood![4] Translated into practical terms, it means that a chi kung practitioner has a more efficient blood flow to supply nutrients to all his cells, as well as a better system to eliminate toxic waste. It also explains why chi kung practitioners do not feel cold so easily, and why they have rosy cheeks.

From the Particle to the Cosmos

Chi kung, which was once taught exclusively to emperors, generals and specially selected disciples, is now available to the public. However, such accessibility is not without its problems. Because chi kung was kept secret for so long, naturally not many people really understand its deeper meanings and wider implications, with the result that it is easy to study and practise it superficially. A person may have spent many years practising chi kung, yet he may not have gone into it deeply because he lacks the philosophical background and the once secretly guarded methodology.

Hence, it is not uncommon for many people to have a partial, superficial understanding of chi kung, often thinking that it is just a system of gentle exercises for some general physical well-being. Shallow learning, of course, occurs in all other disciplines, but it is more lamentable in chi kung, for there is so much chi kung can offer the world.

Chi kung, being the art and science of energy, the stuff which the infinitesimal particle and the infinite galaxies are made of, touches on everything concerning man and the universe. This is not an exaggerated statement: and great chi kung masters actually had deliberated *correctly* on the particle and the cosmos long before modern scientists discovered them.

On a more personal note, chi kung deals with the development of our mind and soul. The mental attainments of Confucianist masters who employed chi kung in their training, for example, are amazing, and they have produced some of the best artistic, scientific and philosophic works of the world. Taoist and Buddhist chi kung have contributed much to spiritual development, providing some practical, effective ways for many people to realize mankind's greatest achievement, that is, spiritual fulfilment, irrespective of their different religions.

Even at the physical level, with which this book is mainly concerned, chi kung is certainly more than just breathing methods and graceful exercise. If you are ready to invest some time and effort, chi kung can give you radiant health and vitality – not just freedom from illness, but more significantly a zest and joy for life.

You will miss a lot of good things if you do not practise chi kung. This book will help you to get better results, and if you wish to know how you can still be young and energetic even at 60, turn to the next chapter and enjoy reading.

2

HOW TO BE YOUNG AND HEALTHY AT SIXTY

The Wonderful Benefits of Chi Kung

❖ *How do some people attain a level of chi kung in six months that it takes others six years to attain?*

Stamina, Agility and Inner Peace

If you think I am joking when I say you can be young and healthy at 60, you are doubly mistaken. Firstly, you can be young and healthy at any age; and, secondly, at 60, by nature's count, one is only middle aged at the most, for man's potential life span is at least 120 years, and woman's is probably longer.

Yes, you can be young and healthy at 60 – if you conscientiously practise the chi kung exercises described in this book, or other chi kung exercises from a competent master. By young, I mean you can carry out most, if not all, of the normal activities young people of 20 can perform, such as having the stamina and agility to run and jump, and the curiosity to look at things with wonder and awe. By healthy, I mean you are not only generally free from illness and pain, but also eat and sleep well, are tolerant of grumbling friends, and often experience a sense of inner peace.

Yes, you can have all these benefits of chi kung, though not by just reading about it, but by consistent, regular practice. This is a small price to pay, compared to the wonderful benefits you will get for life. But before we embark on chi kung practice, which will commence in the next chapter, it is helpful first to examine the aims and objectives of chi kung.

General Aims of Chi Kung

Many people learn chi kung without being clear about their aims and objectives. Such learning, of course, is undirected and wasteful.

There is some difference here between aims and objectives. Aims are general in nature and are spread over a long period, whereas objectives are specific and are measurable within a set time.

For our purpose, we can classify the general aims of chi kung into four main groups, namely health, fitness, longevity and developing our potentials. These aims also correspond to the four main benefits of chi kung. For some people who have attained a fairly high level of personal growth, there is another aim, namely spiritual fulfilment. As this book is mainly concerned with health and vitality, we shall touch on spiritual fulfilment only summarily, and focus on chi kung's more physical aspects.

Chi kung is excellent for curing illness, including so-called 'incurable' diseases, such as hypertension, asthma, insomnia, arthritis, rheumatism, migraine, diabetes, kidney failure and sexual inadequacy. In the course of this book, I shall describe case histories of people who had such 'incurable' diseases, and describe the chi kung exercises many patients practise to be relieved of these diseases.

A more important aspect of chi kung, though it is less obvious, is that it is very effective for preventing illness, and for promoting mental and physical health. This makes chi kung therapy unique. Chi kung cures a person if he is sick; but if he is healthy, the same chi kung exercises will keep him continuously healthy, keeping sickness away!

A healthy person is not necessarily fit, and a fit person is not necessarily healthy! Some sportsmen, who are certainly fit, become seriously ill once they stop their active sports. On the other hand, many healthy persons are not fit: they cannot, for example, run up a flight of stairs without feeling exhausted, nor concentrate on mental work for some time without being fatigued.

To be fit means to have the stamina, endurance and vitality to enjoy work and play. The basic ingredient of fitness is energy. A person who has little energy finds it difficult to enjoy his work or his play; he may even find it hard to stay alive. Chi kung is fundamentally concerned with developing energy; hence, it is obvious that chi kung promotes fitness. If you find that your work, which you used to enjoy, has become a bore, you may have to re-assess your level of fitness. Or if, after returning home from a hard day's work, your wife or husband suggests going out to dinner but you find you lack the energy to comply (though you don't lack the money nor the time), you should start practising chi kung to regain your fitness.

Health and fitness generally, but not necessarily, lead to longevity. On the other hand, it is sad to find that too often people reach a ripe old age, but are neither fit nor healthy. Chi kung ensures longevity *with* health and fitness. If you practise chi kung regularly you will be fit and healthy at 60 and beyond.

Longevity and Personal Growth

How does chi kung ensure longevity? It is helpful, though not complimentary, to use the proverbial analogy of our body and a car. It is even less complimentary, though true, that many of us take better care of our car than our body. If we look after our car well, regularly clean off its dust and rust, oil its parts carefully, and check its functioning regularly so that we don't even have to see a mechanic to correct its faults (because there aren't any faults), then our car is certainly going to give us tip-top performance for a long, long time.

Similarly, if we regularly clean our body of its 'dust and rust', nourish our parts well with energy, and check our physiological functioning regularly with harmonious energy flow so that we don't ever have to see a doctor to correct any malfunctions (because there aren't any malfunctions), then we are certainly going to come close to our potential life span. It is well known that chi kung practitioners, God willing, live long, healthy lives, and this book will show you how.

Most scientists agree that we use only a very small percentage of our abilities and that we have great potentials waiting to be developed. Chi kung is a very good way to develop these latent abilities.

What latent abilities can chi kung bring out? Most of the time we don't know until we have practised long enough for these latent abilities to emerge. But we do know that we can greatly enhance general abilities, as well as the talents or inclinations that we already possess. For example, we can improve our mental focus and our problem solving abilities. One of my students, who encountered many difficulties in his doctorate thesis, overcame his problems quite easily once he had developed a one-pointed mind in his chi kung practice. Another student, a well known pianist, used internal energy flow and meditation to enhance her creativity so successfully that she received numerous standing ovations during her recitals on a continental tour. (*See* p 148–9.)

In developing our potentials, chi kung sometimes brings out psychic or supernormal powers, such as telepathy, clairvoyance, distant healing and control over natural elements. In the past such abilities were regarded as miracles. Many people, including many chi kung students who are unaware of the great depth and extent of chi kung, may find these abilities unbelievable. But I can say with conviction that they are true because some of my disciples, who are perfectly ordinary people, except perhaps in their extraordinary dedication to chi kung, have attained these psychic powers. Nevertheless, while developing our potentials is one of the general aims of chi kung, acquiring these psychic powers is usually not a specific objective of most chi kung students.

Defining Specific Objectives

General aims are meant to be achieved in the long-term and are not easily measurable. For instance, we may aim to improve our health and fitness. If, after practising chi kung, we say goodbye to our previously frequent colds and fevers, and are able to play vigorous games that once we were content just to watch, we can rightly say we have achieved our aims. But it is difficult to measure how much healthier or fitter we have become.

Specific objectives, on the other hand, are set for shorter periods and are usually measurable. For example, we may have an illness and want to practise chi kung to cure ourselves of that illness; or we may frequently feel exhausted and want to improve ourselves so that we can run comfortably round a football field without feeling tired. The needs that we set ourselves to fulfil in this way are our objectives. When setting specific objectives for ourselves it is also advisable to set a suitable period for accomplishing the objectives. At the end of the period, we can categorically measure the success or otherwise of our training in direct reference to our objectives.

The kind of specific objectives we define for ourselves depends on our own needs, as well as on the course of chi kung we practise. Hence, we can classify objectives into two groups, namely personal objectives and course objectives. Personal objectives are those that concern our personal needs, such as curing a particular disease or acquiring psychic powers; while course objectives are those that are defined by specific courses, such as dynamic chi kung or abdominal breathing.

The following are some examples of personal objectives:

1 Cure a particular illness.
2 Increase stamina so as to enjoy games.
3 Enhance martial art abilities.
4 Improve concentration and endurance in work.
5 Enhance mental freshness and perception.
6 Improve sexual performance.
7 Practise some non-vigorous exercises for health and fitness.
8 Increase or reduce weight.
9 Manage stress.
10 Increase knowledge of and ability in chi kung.
11 Acquire psychic powers.
12 Develop spiritually.

The above examples will give us some suggestions to help us decide on our own personal objectives. Obviously, we need to be reasonable in our objectives, and give ourselves adequate time – at least a few months – to realize them. We can then evaluate how successful we have been in accomplishing our objectives after this set time.

Objectives of Different Chi Kung Types

Different types or courses of chi kung will each have their own objectives. There are four main categories of, or approaches to, chi kung, namely dynamic chi kung, self-manifested chi movement (or induced chi flow), quiescent chi kung and meditation. These approaches will be discussed in some detail in Chapter 8, and every approach is represented by some examples in this book. Here, only a brief description of their specific objectives is given; readers will have a better perspective of these objectives after they have read the relevant chapters.

Dynamic chi kung is represented in this book by ten Shaolin Dynamic Chi Kung Patterns, with the following specific objectives.

1 Loosen and strengthen muscles and joints.
2 Increase agility and flexibility.
3 Use particular patterns to cure particular illnesses.
4 Use particular patterns to train certain skills or forces.
5 Use the whole set of ten patterns for holistic development of the body.
6 Used selected patterns as means to induce chi flow.

Self-manifested chi movement (or induced chi flow) is a generic term referring to a group of chi kung exercises whereby the practitioner induces energy to flow inside his body, resulting in self-manifested movements. This genre of chi kung is represented in this book by Shaolin Cosmos Self-Manifested Chi Movement, with the following specific objectives.

1 Experience chi flowing inside the body.
2 Enjoy flowing meditation.
3 Cleanse the body of dust and rust.
4 Clear blockages in meridians.
5 Harmonize energy flow.
6 Balance energy levels in the body.

There are many excellent breathing methods in chi kung. Abdominal Breathing, with its specific objectives listed below, is one fundamental method.

1 Focus the body's centre of gravity at the abdomen so as to achieve better balance.
2 Tap cosmic energy and store it at the abdominal energy field for later use.
3 Increase vital energy.
4 Create a pearl of energy to be radiated centrifugally to all parts of the body, or to be circulated round the body in a 'small universal chi flow'.

5 Merge energy with mind, to attain a unity of body and spirit.

Meditation, in various forms, is an integral part of chi kung that many students are not aware of. Standing Meditation and Sitting Meditation are presented in this book, and they have the following objectives.

1 Attain deep relaxation.
2 Reach a 'chi kung state of mind' which is at a deeper level than our normal level of consciousness.
3 Achieve a one-pointed mind.
4 Attain clarity of thought.
5 Perform creative visualization.
6 Enter a state of mind whereby we can be energized by cosmic energy.
7 Experience the void.
8 Attain spiritual fulfilment.

Some of these objectives, such as attaining a unity of body and spirit, and being energized by the cosmos, are advanced chi kung. So, if you are at the elementary or intermediate stage, do not be worried if you find these objectives puzzling.

Useful Advice to Students

How do some people attain a level of chi kung in six months that it takes others six years to attain? Indeed, it is regrettable that many practitioners have spent years practising chi kung diligently (and mistakenly believe themselves to have reached a master's level) yet they remain at the elementary stage! This reminds us of the advice: 'it's not enough to practise hard; practise smart'.

   One important factor in practising smart in chi kung is to have a sound basic understanding of its meaning and scope, as well as of the general aims and specific objectives of the training. If we think of chi kung as just some form of gentle exercise, and mock sincere teachers when they explain that chi kung spans the minute particle and the infinite cosmos, then at the most we will only attain good health even though we may practise chi kung for a lifetime. Our philosophical concept of our discipline necessarily influences the methodology we choose and the results we attain.

Having a clear idea of our aims and objectives, and reassessing our progress periodically, is imperative if we wish to achieve maximum results in minimum time. It is indeed lamentable that so many people waste a lot of time because they have no direction or set purpose in their practice. Most of those who have spent years practising chi kung yet have accomplished little, are hardly aware of the direction their practice is leading, nor of the fascinating potentialities chi kung can offer them. This is probably because of their dogged adherence to their conservative routine, a misguided belief that their school or method is superior, or lack of exposure to good masters or enlightening literature. 'Be humble in the quest for knowledge' has always been good advice.

Before starting a programme of chi kung training, we should define both our general aims and our specific objectives. We may aim, for example, to improve our health and vitality. If we have a particular illness, such as diabetes or asthma, curing this illness is obviously one of the specific objectives.

If we are not clinically sick, we may have to do some self examination to decide which specific aspect of health or vitality we want to accomplish. It is not sufficient to say: I want to be healthier and more energetic – this will be a general aim. Some examples of specific objectives could be: I want to be able to sleep soundly five minutes after lying in bed every night; I want not to be irritated the next time my boss or subordinate differs from me; I want to play a game of badminton without feeling exhausted. Unlike general aims, specific objectives are such that we can easily tell whether we have succeeded or not after our set period of chi kung practice.

Just as we have to be reasonable in our aims and objectives, we have to be reasonable in the time we set ourselves to accomplish them. If you have been suffering from migraine or peptic ulcers for years, it is unreasonable and unrealistic to expect to be cured after a few chi kung practice sessions. If professional boxers have spent years training to fight, do not expect to beat them in the ring just because you practise chi kung – though chi kung will actually develop your power and stamina and will improve your chance of beating them if you are already well versed in boxing.

Since it takes only seven months for nature to replace all the cells in our body, we can reasonably conclude that, if everything works out ideally, all physical diseases can be cured within this time. Hence, giving ourselves some allowance, it is fair to expect that if we practise the right type of chi kung therapy conscientiously, and if we do not do silly things to aggravate the disease during recovery, all physical illness can be cured in one year. The experiences of my students show that generally insomnia can be cured in two months, hypertension in six, and rheumatism in nine.

Having set our aims and defined our objectives, the logical step is to find a master, select the appropriate techniques, then practise regularly and consistently.

The Three Essentials in Chi Kung Training

Chi kung is scientific. If we follow certain chi kung methods and practise adequately, we will derive the expected result. For example, a certain chi kung therapeutic technique is known to cure a particular disease, so if we practise this technique diligently for the required length of time we will be relieved of the disease. If we do not achieve the expected result, as sometimes happens, then something has gone wrong along the way. This something wrong can be traced to problems in three main areas, known as the three essentials of chi kung training, namely the method, the master and the student.

Obviously, if we do not use the right method, we will not get the desired result. If we ever achieve the desired result despite a poor method, it is accidental and happens only after a much longer period. Although good chi kung methods were jealously guarded secrets in the past, they are now readily available.

But even if we know the method, we need a master who will not only instruct us, but, more significantly, will also explain finer or individual points that are too difficult or impractical to be explained in books. The supervision of a master is also essential to correct our mistakes and to provide remedial exercises should we develop deviations. It is dangerous to practise advanced chi kung without a master's supervision. However, if a master is not available, a good book may be a poor substitute, especially if we are already familiar with chi kung and the exercises are not advanced.

But the most important essential is the student. We may have the best method and the best master, but if we are not ready or able to practise correctly and regularly, we are not likely to get a good result, and sometimes may not get any result. What the student has to do is apparently very simple: follow the master's advice, and practise, practise, practise. In reality, this is most difficult for most students. Insufficient practice is the main reason why many students do not attain outstanding results even though they are blessed with the rare opportunity of having a good master.

A Chinese proverb says: 'To find a good master is difficult; to find a good student is even more difficult'. It is commonly said that masters always keep some secrets to themselves, fearing that their students may be better than them. This is a very unfair statement which appears to be valid to uninitiated people. While the statement may be true for some, most masters are in fact very eager to pass on their arts to their students. This is a fact I have personally learnt from my experience with many chi kung and kungfu masters.

It is almost always the students who falter. Because the students fail to practise sufficiently to attain the required standard, the master cannot proceed further. If he does he can merely explain to the students the techniques which he hopes they may one day practise, but which they virtually never will; and the students will not be able to acquire the abilities or skills that qualify them to become masters in their turn. Most people, often including the students themselves, erroneously think that the master has kept the final secrets. The pain the master feels in his heart – not because of this misunderstanding nor the unfair judgement other people pass on him (most masters are great enough not to be bothered with such trifles), but because of the tremendous disappointment that the students he has so arduously, sometimes selflessly, nurtured, fail in their endeavour – often lies too deep for words.

3

ENJOY THE POETRY OF HEALTH AND VITALITY

Introduction to Dynamic Chi Kung Patterns

❖ *Chi Kung is basically an internal art; the outward forms and movements are external aids to internal cultivation.*

Having acquainted ourselves with some basic knowledge of chi kung, we are now ready to embark on an interesting journey – the poetic journey of health and vitality. From now on, we shall be doing a lot of practical work, we shall be practising some of the patterns that, in the past, masters kept exclusively for their selected students.

These chi kung patterns have helped literally thousands of people to be relieved of their so-called incurable diseases, such as hypertension, asthma, ulcers, rheumatism, arthritis, kidney failure, diabetes, migraine and insomnia. But, of course, neither the author nor the publisher, nor the best doctor, nor anyone else can guarantee you a definite cure. We can only provide a proven way; you yourself have to travel on it. We can only show the methods; you have to practise them correctly. But we can help you much by giving you guidance and relevant advice.

If you are not sick, these exercises will also be very beneficial to you – personally, I think they will even be more beneficial. Great masters of Chinese medicine throughout the ages have always emphasized that 'superior medicine prevents diseases, inferior medicine cures them.' These exercises, which have been selected from among the best in chi kung, do even more than prevent illness; they actively promote radiant physical, emotional and mental health – if you perform them correctly and regularly.

Practising these exercises correctly and regularly is a crucial factor in achieving good results. Some students do not benefit as much as expected, because they falter on this factor. Of the two aspects – correct practice and regular practice – the second is even more important. You need not strive for perfect exactness; in fact, you are advised not to, because worrying too much about whether you are performing the exercises correctly or not becomes a stress on your mind. Some margin of allowance for individual differences and shortcomings is always permissible in all the exercises.

But you do have to practise regularly. There is no escape from this rule. There is a saying that 'every unit of progress is the result of every unit of effort'. It is best to practise once in the morning and once in the evening or at night, for about 15 to 30 minutes per session. If you practise only once a day (for about 15 to 30 minutes), that is quite sufficient. It is permissible – but not recommended – to miss one or more sessions once in a while, as long as your overall practice is regular. But if you practise daily, say, for a month, then stop for half a month, and subsequently continue off and on, you are not likely to get good results.

It is preferable to have an instructor to supervise you, even if he is not an instructor of the same type of chi kung. Much of chi kung is internal, delicate and profound – aspects that are best learnt from personal instruction, and are not easy to be explained in books. Hence, if you are a beginner, I would strongly advise you to seek a good chi kung master.

Shaolin Wahnam Chi Kung Patterns

The following ten dynamic chi kung patterns have greatly benefited many students in our chi kung school, the Shaolin Wahnam Chi Kung Institute. Our school is named 'Shaolin' because we practise the type of chi kung that originated from the Shaolin Monastery of China, regarded as 'the foremost monastery beneath heaven', from where Shaolin Kungfu and Zen Buddhism also originated. It is named 'Wahnam', in honour of my two masters, Lai Chin Wah and Ho

Fatt Nam, who so generously and kindly passed on the Shaolin arts to me.

You may practise the ten patterns individually, in the sequence shown in the book, in shorter sequences of three or four selected patterns, or in any way you like. In later chapters, you will learn how to draw on this repertoire to devise your own programmes to serve particular needs, such as curing a specific illness, managing stress, increasing stamina, or enjoying deep relaxation. Many students, because they have insufficient knowledge of chi kung principles, are naturally apprehensive about modifying the techniques they have learnt from their masters. This is understandable, as wrong practice may lead to harmful side-effects. But once you know some basic principles, you will find that chi kung exercises are very versatile and full of fun.

Lifting the Sky

This is one of the best exercises in chi kung, and thus it is found in many styles. It is easy to practise, yet its benefits, if you persist in your training, are marvellous.

Lim, aged 27, a shopkeeper in Gurun, had suffered from haemorrhoids for many years. (For ethical and other reasons, fictitious names are used in the examples given in this and other chapters, though the case histories are genuine.) Lim was about to undergo a surgical operation to remove his piles, when he decided to give chi kung a try, though, like many young men, he was initially sceptical about its effectiveness. But after about six months of chi kung, his haemorrhoids disappeared.

This Lifting the Sky exercise is the main one I asked him to practise. I also asked him, as he pushed up his hands to lift the sky, to lift his piles back into their rightful cavity. I know it works because I had a similar problem 25 years ago. My master, Sifu Ho Fatt Nam, taught me the same chi kung exercise to overcome my problem.

Of course you do not need to have haemorrhoids to enjoy this exercise. In fact, curing haemorrhoids is a comparatively minor, auxiliary function of this wonderful exercise. Its main function is to promote overall energy flow in the body. It is a very good introductory exercise for any chi kung training.

Stand with your feet fairly close together, with your arms hanging effortlessly at your sides. Give yourself a few seconds to feel relaxed. Then smile from your heart. Don't worry how you do it; just do it. Just smile from your heart and feel, really feel, how relaxed, cheerful and happy you are. It is a big mistake to think I am being farcical. But I can tell you, in my capacity as a chi kung grandmaster, that this feeling of relaxation and cheerfulness from your heart may possibly be the best benefit of this exercise.

Then place your hands in the position shown in Figure 3.1(a), with the fingers almost touching each other, your wrists at right angles to your arms, and your arms straight. You will probably feel some slight tension in your wrists and arms.

With the wrists still at right angles and elbows straight, move your arms forwards and then upwards in a continuous arc. Simultaneously, breathe in gently through the nose. I repeat, *gently*. This is of the utmost importance: never, never force your breathing.

As you breathe in gently, visualize invigorating cosmic energy flowing into you. The visualization must be done gently, very gently. If you find difficulty visualizing, that doesn't matter. Leave out the visualization for the time being, and just give yourself a gentle thought that good cosmic energy is flowing into you. Just a gentle thought will do.

When you reach the position shown in Figure 3.1(b), hold your action and your breath for a second or two. Then push up, as if pushing or 'lifting' the sky. Your arms should be straight and your wrists at right angles to your arms.

Then lower your arms to your sides in a continuous arc, like a bird flapping its wings, Figure 3.1(c). The arms should be straight, and the hands and forearms should now be in the same plane. Simultaneously breathe out gently through the mouth.

As you breathe out, gently visualize negative energy being sent away. Negative energy can be translated as carbon dioxide, or toxic waste, or your illness, or your bad emotions, or any rubbish that you do not want. You may, if you like, just give yourself a gentle thought instead of visualizing.

Fig 3.1(a), (b), (c)   Lifting the Sky

This completes one round of the exercise. If you are practising this exercise by itself, perform 20 to 30 rounds; if you are practising it in combination with two or three other exercises, perform about ten rounds; if you are practising it as one of the sequence of ten exercises, perform four to eight rounds. These figures are, however, just guidelines; practise as many times as you wish.

Plucking Stars

After Lifting the Sky, let us perform Plucking Stars. Cheong, aged 65, was a coffee shop assistant in my hometown, Sungai Petani. He had been advised thrice by his surgeon (who also learned chi kung from me later on) to have an operation to remove his injured duodenum, as he had been suffering from duodenal ulcers for many years. Cheong did not go for the operation, partly because of his age, and mainly because the honest surgeon told him that even if the operation was successful (and it normally was), there was no guarantee that there might not be a relapse of the same illness.

Cheong took up chi kung instead. Of the various Shaolin dynamic patterns he did, Plucking Stars was the one he emphasized most, because it is particularly effective for the stomach and abdominal regions. As he progressed in his chi kung practice, he gradually phased out his medication and after about six months no longer needed to take any pills. We could follow his case closely because it so happened that his chi kung instructor was also the supervisor of the hospital where he received treatment. This happened many years ago, since then he has had only one relapse, when he had to do more chi kung exercises to overcome the pain.

Previously, if you gently tapped his stomach, Cheong would bend double with pain. Now you can punch his stomach – we actually tried that – without causing him any discomfort. But the most interesting thing is that Cheong, who was pale, weak and fragile a few years ago, now feels and looks younger than his 30-year-old son.

To pluck stars, stand upright and relaxed, with your feet fairly close together. Place your open palms in front of you at your stomach level as if holding a huge ball, Figure 3.2(a) – actually you are holding a ball of chi or cosmic energy, invisible to ordinary eyes, but real. Simultaneously, gently breathe through your nose into your abdomen, and visualize or simply think of cosmic energy flowing into you. If you cannot perform abdominal breathing (*see* p 76) yet, then breathe naturally.

Lift your lower hand upwards, turning the hand in the process, so that the open palm pushes up towards the sky

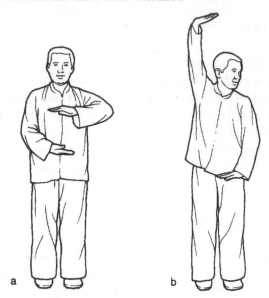

Fig 3.2(a), (b)   Plucking Stars

directly above your head, while your other hand presses directly down near your groin with the open palm towards the ground. Both arms should be straight, and the fingers of both hands should point inward. Breathe out gently through your mouth, and visualize or think of energy flowing to your two hands, Figure 3.2 (b).

Next bring your two hands towards each other to hold a ball, as at the start of the exercise except that the positions of your upper and lower hands are now reversed. Breathe in gently and visualize cosmic energy flowing in.

Repeat the procedure 20 to 30 times if you are practising this exercise alone; about ten times in combination with two or three other exercises; or about six times as one of the sequence of ten dynamic exercises.

This Plucking Stars exercise is not only effective in curing ulcers; it is effective against disorders of the stomach and spleen systems, including gastritis, indigestion, diabetes, liver and gall bladder problems. Of course, one does not have to be sick to benefit from this exercise. All chi kung exercises are preventive as well as curative, and have other fascinating benefits as well as their value in treating medical problems. The Plucking Stars exercise also opens up meridians (or pathways of energy flow) at the sides of our body, promoting the function of some of these meridians as energy reservoirs (see p 82).

Some readers may find it odd that a therapeutic exercise that cures gastritis can also be effective against an ailment caused by the opposite conditions, indigestion. This problem is only relevant when considered in terms of Western chemotherapy, where a particular drug is used to cure a particular illness. In chi kung therapy, which is based on a totally different medical philosophy, the problem is irrelevant. Chinese medical principles will be discussed in Chapter 13; here it suffices to say that the purpose of the exercise is to promote harmonious energy flow to the respective systems or organs to restore their natural functions, so that just the right amount of gastric juices will be produced according to the amount of food, or lack of it, in the stomach.

If you just perform this and other dynamic chi kung exercises, without appropriate breath control and visualization, as many uninformed students do, you will at best derive only those benefits pertaining to gentle exercise. You will have missed the most significant benefits of chi kung, such as harmonious energy flow engendered by breath control, and the effect of mind over matter operated by creative visualization.

It must be emphasized again that chi kung is not just some form of gentle exercise, as many students erroneously imagine. If it were, more benefits would be obtained from such physical exercises as gymnastics, body-building and aerobics. Chi kung is basically an internal art; the outward forms and movements are external aids to internal cultivation. We shall look at more dynamic chi kung exercises in the next chapter, where we shall learn to develop internal energy to push mountains and carry the moon!

4

THE ENERGY TO PUSH MOUNTAINS AND CARRY THE MOON

Continuation of Dynamic Chi Kung Patterns

❖ *The mind factor is, in many ways, the most important aspect of chi kung.*

Gentle but Powerful

If you have read or heard of kungfu stories, you will probably have come across tales of beautiful ladies, who are gentle and fragile looking but have skilful and powerful fighting abilities. Many people will think that these are only stories, and find it hard to imagine how a lady can be powerful without losing at least some of her gentleness and (apparent) fragility, just as they find it difficult to believe the fantastic feats some chi kung masters can perform.

But I can verify this: a lady, or any gentle person (unless he is very young, old or sick), can develop enough power to break a brick without losing any of his or her gentleness – and without having to undergo rough conditioning like striking poles or hitting sandbags. How? By practising chi kung, of course. And we are going to learn a very useful technique for this purpose in this chapter. Not only can a lady retain her lady-like qualities, she can also actually become more beautiful and lively, because by harmonizing energy flow and promoting mental freshness, chi kung makes her skin glow and her eyes sparkle.

When some of my lady students had developed sufficient internal force, I told them they could break bricks with their bare hands. Almost no one could believe it, and when I gave them some bricks to break, no one could do so. Then I demonstrated how I could break one, and showed them that my hands are also soft and gentle like theirs. I encouraged them to try, showing them individually the finer points of the breaking technique, such as the position of their feet, the turning of their waist and the swing of their arms. Once one succeeded in breaking a brick, the others soon succeeded too.

This development of power and testing it on breaking a brick also illustrates two significant points. Firstly, it illustrates the importance of having a master's personal instruction. Although the ladies had the required power, without my detailed explanation of the finer points, and the confidence I instilled in them by my demonstration with my equally gentle hands – both of these factors cannot be easily described in books – they would not have been able to break the bricks.

The Importance of Mind

Secondly, this brick-breaking example illustrates the utmost importance of our mind. At first the ladies could not break the bricks because they believed they could not do it. Later, inspired by the ease of my demonstration, when they believed they could, they succeeded. We may have the potential ability, including the required techniques, but if we assume, consciously or unconsciously, that what we set out to do is impossible, then we will fail. But if we have the right attitude, and believe in what we are doing, we will succeed. There is much truth in the saying of the great mystic masters that 'What our mind can believe; we can achieve'.

The mind factor is, in many ways, the most important aspect of chi kung. Most chi kung students are not bothered with breaking bricks; if they need to break one, it is so much easier to use a hammer or just drop it onto hard ground. This brick-breaking example is mentioned because it illustrates very clearly the importance of having the right attitude in chi kung training, of having the right frame of mind. If, for example, we have doubt as we practise a particular chi kung technique to cure some illness, we will greatly minimize our chance of recovery. But, inspired by the knowledge that many others have been cured by the same technique, if we practise with confidence and faith, we will maximize our chance of success.

This, of course, does not suggest that we should follow blindly whatever is told to us. While we should be open-minded, we must also be aware of bogus chi kung instructors. Indeed, an important principle of Shaolin philosophy advises that we should not accept anything on faith or reputation alone, but should practise diligently with an open mind and then assess the teaching based on our personal experience.

Pushing Mountains

Pushing Mountains is a deceptively simple chi kung pattern used by Shaolin monks to develop internal force at their arms and palms. If you are interested in martial arts, but not interested in banging poles and sandbags to harden your arms and palms, you will find Pushing Mountains is useful.

It is also beneficial for those suffering from arthritis, rheumatism, kidney problems and back pain. If you wonder how this Pushing Mountains, which principally involves arm movements, can affect other parts of the body, the answer is that because of the extensive network of meridians (see p 80), vital energy is stimulated to flow to and from the arms, through various organs in the body and down the legs.

Sharifah is a young, pretty lady who can break a brick although she has never done any hard-conditioning exercises. Pushing Mountains is one of the dynamic chi kung exercises that she spent much time on, not because she wanted to have brick-breaking palms – in fact, this idea never occurred to her – but because she wanted to cure her chronic back pain which she had suffered since she was a child. She informed me she had consulted as many doctors as she could meet, but they could not find anything physically wrong with her. I told her that many of the meridians at her back were blocked, resulting in 'packets' of energy blockage which are too minute to be detected by conventional Western instruments. After about four months of daily chi kung she had cleared the blockages and the pain disappeared.

Fig 4.1(a), (b)   Pushing Mountains

Stand with your feet close together. Place your two palms, fingers pointing upward, at breast level at the sides of your body, with your two elbows pointing to the back, Figure 4.1(a). Breathe in gently, and visualize (or think of) cosmic energy flowing into you.

Gently push out both hands. Breathe out and visualize your vital energy flowing from your back to your palms, Figure 4.1(b).

Then bring both hands back to the starting position at breast level, breathing in at the same time. Repeat this procedure 30 to 50 times if you are practising this pattern by itself; or any suitable number of times if you combine it with other patterns.

During your practice, when you feel that energy is flowing through your arms, close your eyes and imagine a mountain in front of you. As you push out, and gently breathe out, feel that your energy is so powerful that you are pushing the mountain away. Do not use any strength; let your chi do the work.

As you bring back your hands, and breathe in, you can choose one of these two alternatives. If you like the mountain, you can play with it, drawing it back with your withdrawing hands, then pushing it away as you push out your palms. Alternatively, give the mountain a break as you pull back your hands, and think of yourself being charged with more cosmic energy. Push the mountain away as you push out. In this way the mountain will be pushed farther and farther away until it disappears from sight.

Carrying the Moon

While Pushing Mountains will increase your internal force, Carrying the Moon will enhance your youthfulness. If you wish to be young and healthy at 60 and beyond, practise this exercise every day.

Carrying the Moon will give you a supple spine, which is extremely important for good health, because many vital nerves issue from here. A supple spine is essential if we want to be alert physically as well as mentally. There is a Chinese saying that 'You need not worry about growing old, so long as your spine is young'.

Young people are generally concerned with sex, though most are prudent enough not to discuss it openly. In Chinese medical philosophy, the kidney is the most important organ responsible for sexual vitality. Many people, including many Chinese themselves, may be puzzled at how the kidneys could be related to sex, but recent discoveries in Western science have shown that there is a connection between the kidneys and the pituitary gland, which in turn is linked to the production of sperm or ova in the respective sex organs. Carrying the Moon massages and strengthens the kidneys, thus enhancing sexual vitality.

This exercise also gives some hope to balding men. David was getting bald at 50. He did this exercise conscientiously every morning and night, both for his kidneys and his balding head. We did not ask him about his sexual vitality, but everyone could see that after about eight months of practising chi kung hair began to grow on his head!

From the ordinary upright standing position, bend your body forward so that your hands drop just below your knees, Figure 4.2(a). Tuck your head in so that your whole back makes a smooth curve. Pause in this poise for a few seconds, and visualize vital energy flowing up your spine to your head. You may feel some pulsation at baihui, the vital point at the crown of your head. If you are keen to

Fig 4.2(a), (b), (c)   Carrying the Moon

have more hair on your head, focus on and enjoy this pulsation for some time.

Bring your body and gently straightened arms forward and upward in a continuous movement, gently breathing in simultaneously, until you reach the highest extent, then form with your thumbs and index fingers the shape of a full moon above and behind your head, arching your back and your head backward, Figure 4.2(b). Then hold the poise and your breathing for a few seconds while looking at the moon formed by your fingers.

Straighten your body and lower your arms to the sides, breathing out gently, Figure 4.2(c). At the same time, visualize vital energy flowing from your head downward in all directions like an internal shower, cleansing away all your dust and rust, and flowing away as negative energy into the ground. If you are a conscientious environmentalist, don't worry that this may pollute the earth: what is negative energy to you can be nutrients to other living things in the ground. Repeat the process as many times as needed.

This internal shower of energy is the most beautiful part of the exercise. Virtually all my students enjoy this cascade of energy tingling down their body.

Circulating Head

We can enjoy not only energy tingling down our body, but also tingling inside our head! Circulating Head is one exercise that can achieve such an effect.

Stand upright and relaxed, with your feet fairly close together. Clear your mind of all thoughts and be cheerful. Then turn your head horizontally to one side as far back as you can without discomfort. Try to look farther back with your eyes than your head can turn. Do not worry about your breathing. Throughout this Circulating Head exercise let your breathing be spontaneous. Then slowly and gracefully turn your head to the other side, Figure 4.3(a). Repeat about three times. It is not important whether you start turning to your left or your right side.

Then move your head vertically up and down about three times, Figure 4.3(b). Perform the movement slowly and gracefully. When you turn your head down, try to touch your chest with your chin, without moving your back. When you turn your head up, try to tilt your head as far back as you comfortably can, with your eyes looking even farther back. Do not worry about your breathing.

Next gently circulate your head in as big a circle as you can without discomfort, making sure you rotate your head back enough, but without moving your shoulders, Figure 4.3(c). You can start with either side, and circulate about three times before changing to the other direction. Breathe naturally.

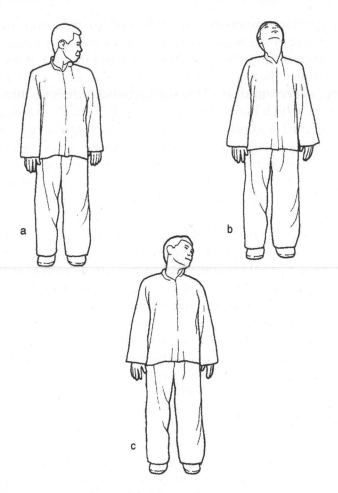

Fig 4.3(a), (b), (c)   Circulating Head

After you have done all these horizontal, vertical and rotating movements, keep still, close your eyes, and let go of everything. If you have done this exercise correctly and have practised sufficiently, you may feel energy massaging your scalp, like when you are shampooing your hair, or you may feel energy tingling pleasantly inside your head. However, should you feel giddy or develop a headache, you should stop the exercise, and may continue another time with care. Those with hypertension must perform this exercise cautiously.

Some important functions are achieved in this exercise. The gentle turning of the head loosens the muscles of the neck, which is the vital connection between the head and the rest of the body. This promotes better circulation of blood and vital energy, including nerve impulses. This turning also indirectly affects the spinal cord, which hangs down from the base of the head, giving the spinal cord a gentle shake-up and sending energy tingling down the spinal column. Fourthly, this exercise focuses energy at the head, clearing blockages and nourishing brain cells. By understanding these vital functions, you will no longer be amazed at what an apparently simple exercise can do – if it is done properly.

This exercise is very useful in relieving ailments related to the head, such as frequent giddiness, headache, migraine, nervousness, mental fatigue, slow responses, as well as stiff neck and low blood pressure. Henry, a manager of an international company, suffered from migraine and a host of other ailments which he had developed while working hard to make his business successful. He specially liked this exercise as it enabled him to enjoy pleasant tingling sensations in his head. Sometimes he saw colourful lights flashing internally. As he progressed in his chi kung training, his health gradually improved.

But once, after practising Circulating Head, his migraine, which had become less frequent, came back intensely. I told him that possibly this was 'chi uprooting the cause of his illness', whereby vital energy was making a thorough attempt to clear some blockages deep inside his head. His reply was both interesting and courageous. He said, 'I've tolerated this pain for years; I might as well tolerate it for another month to allow chi some time to do the cleansing'. Sure enough, after about a month of frequent intense pain, his migraine disappeared, and has never returned since.

Merry-Go-Round

When I was a small boy, my mother frequently took me to a merry-go-round, which was always an exhilarating experience. Now I teach my students to do their own Merry-Go-Round, which is specially exhilarating if they have been sitting for hours at office work. This exercise is also very useful in relieving backache, rheumatism, diabetes and indigestion, as well as indirectly helping to cure many other ailments.

Radha, aged 42, a financial comptroller of an international corporation, frequently felt tired and sleepy when in his office. This Merry-Go-Round, he told me, was an excellent tonic: all he needed was to close his office door, do a few swings, and he would feel fresh again and ready to look at figures. I added that the next time he felt sleepy during his frequent long distance drives, he did not have to stop his car and do a 100 metre jog, as recommended by some road safety experts; he still had to stop his car, but he could do the Merry-Go-Round instead. This advice, however, was not necessary, for a few months later, he told me that he felt as fresh as a mountain stream.

For the Merry-Go-Round exercise, stand with your feet about two shoulder widths apart, bend your knees and sit down (on air) onto a horse-riding stance. Bend your body forward and clasp the fingers of your two hands, Figure 4.4(a).

With your arms fairly straight, and your fingers clasped together, rotate your body at the waist with your outstretched arms drawing a big circle, Figure 4.4(b). It does not matter whether you start from your left or right, but you must make sure that you rotate as far back as you comfortably can. Remember you are doing a merry-go-round, not a fairy wheel. Breathe in gently as you rotate the first half of the big circle.

As you reach about the mid-point of your backward rotation, but without any break in your circular movement, breathe out gently, Figure 4.4(c). Continue the movement until you come back to your starting point. Pause for a second or two. Then repeat the process in the *same* direction. Perform the exercise about three times in the same direction, before repeating the same number of times in the other direction.

Abdominal breathing is used in this exercise, but if you are not familiar with abdominal breathing yet (see p 76), just breathe naturally. In the process of circulating your body, visualize (or think of) energy radiating from your mingmen, the vital point at the middle of your waist at the back, to all parts of your skeletal framework.

Fig 4.4(a), (b), (c)   Merry-Go-Round

All these dynamic chi kung exercises can be practised individually or in combination with other chi kung exercises, dynamic or otherwise. A rough guide is to perform each dynamic exercise about 20 times to 30 times if it is to be practised on its own, except Pushing Mountains which can be performed more times, and Circulating Head and Merry-Go-Round which are not normally practised more than five times. If you wish to practise all the six patterns that we have learnt, a rough guide is to perform each pattern about four to eight times.

5

BENEFITING FROM THE ART OF LONGEVITY

Conclusion of Dynamic Chi Kung Patterns

❖ *If we wish to live healthy, long lives, and to have vitality to enjoy our work and play, chi kung is an excellent answer.*

Big Windmill

Chi kung is actually a modern term, referring to various arts of developing energy for specific purposes. In the past these arts were known by different names, such as the Art of Health, the Art of Longevity and the Art of Internal Strength. Hence, if we wish to live healthy, long lives, and to have vitality to enjoy our work and play, chi kung is an excellent answer. In the previous two chapters, we learnt interesting exercises with poetic names like Plucking Stars and Merry-Go-Round; here we complete the ten Shaolin Dynamic Chi Kung Patterns, beginning with Big Windmill.

Stand at the usual ready position with feet together, cheerful heart and empty mind, letting your arms hang loosely at your sides, with your open palms facing the back (*see* Figure 5.3(d)). Circle one arm in a continuous forward, upward and backward movement, like a big windmill, Figure 5.1(a). Keep your palm open, and your elbow straight but not locked. Breathe in gently as your arm is moving forward and upward.

There are two methods of breath control you can use: chest breathing and abdominal breathing. Chest breathing

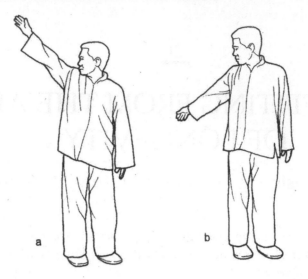

Fig 5.1(a), (b)   Big Windmill

is more 'forceful', and is preferred if the purpose is to develop powerful arms and palms. It is therefore favoured in martial art chi kung. Abdominal breathing is more 'gentle', and is preferred if the purpose is to cure or nourish certain organs in the body. It is favoured in medical chi kung. Whether you use chest or abdominal breathing, the breathing must be gentle, never forced.

When you breathe in visualize (or think of) cosmic energy flowing into your chest if you use chest breathing, or into your abdomen if you use abdominal breathing. As your arm continues its backward and downward movement, breathe out gently, Figure 5.1 (b). For chest breathing, visualize energy flowing through your arm, elbow, wrist and palm into your fingers. For abdominal breathing, visualize energy massaging, cleansing and strengthening various organs in your abdomen. If you have a particular medical problem, such as hardened liver or diabetes, think gently of the relevant organ, in this case the liver or the pancreas.

When you have completed the circular arm movement, turn your palm to face backward as in the ready position. Pause like this for two or three seconds to feel the tingling sensation in your fingers, or the massaging effect on your organs. Repeat the process with the same arm for an appropriate number of times before changing to the other arm.

Mrs Chen, an energetic 36-year-old woman who looked after her family business, had suffered from diabetes for about five years. She had to take medicine every day. After a few weeks of chi kung practice, I advised her to take Sunday off from her daily medication. In her typically business-like manner she monitored her sugar level every day. After two weeks, as she felt that missing her Sunday medication had not affected her significantly, she took another pill-free holiday. After another two weeks she took three days off without pills. In this way, she was free from pills after about five months, yet her sugar level was normal. But she dared not take as much sugar as she would like.

I told her that if she had to control her sugar intake, it meant she had not fully recovered. To be cured means to be able to carry on our daily life normally, including taking our normal amount of food without any need for strict control. If we are healthy, I explained, our body will naturally produce the right amount and the right types of chemicals to neutralize the excessive sugar, fat, calcium or whatever in our systems. I advised Mrs Chen to add just a little bit more sugar to her drinks every three days, but reminded her that she must not neglect her chi kung practice. After another three months, she could take as much sugar as she wished without any fear of relapsing into diabetes. She said that the Big Windmill not only cured her of her diabetes, but also made her arms strong so that she could carry heavy goods in her business.

Hula-Hoop

The Hula-Hoop is another chi kung exercise that looks simple but has tremendous benefits. Indeed the outward form is easy, but most of the benefits are derived from the inner aspects of energy flow and visualization. Failing to appreciate this important point is a major reason why many students obtain only minimal results from their chi kung training.

Stand at the ready position. Rub your palms together to make them warm, then place them behind your back over

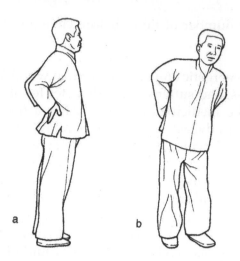

Fig 5.2(a), (b)   Hula-Hoop

your kidney region. Close your eyes and visualize energy flowing from your palms into your kidneys, Figure 5.2(a). Repeat this a few times. Next, with your palms over your kidney region, rotate your hips as if doing a hula-hoop dance, about 20 to 30 rounds, visualizing energy massaging, cleansing and strengthening your kidneys, Figure 5.2(b). Rotate in the other direction about the same number of times.

Then stand upright, relax fully, drop your hands to your sides, close your eyes (if they are not already closed), and enjoy the tingling or massaging sensation at your kidneys or any other parts of your body. If you continue to rotate or move in any way without your volition, do not resist the momentum but let yourself go completely and enjoy the involuntary movement. If this involuntary movement does not occur, it does not matter; just stand still and enjoy the massaging sensation.

If the movement starts to be vigorous, just tell yourself to slow down. You will find that you can control the movement with your mind. You may find this surprising but it is actually a natural ability, a fact great chi kung masters have known since ancient times. The trouble is that some people do not believe this is true.

The kidneys, in Chinese medical philosophy, are not only important for sexual vitality, but also for the general vitality of the whole body. The kidney system is directly related to the urinary bladder system, and also affects bones and muscles. This Hula-Hoop exercise is effective against many medical complaints, and is particularly beneficial to those suffering from kidney and urinary bladder problems, sexual inadequacy, impotence, infertility, and general infirmity.

Mrs Ong had been married for many years but was still childless, though she and her husband had tried very hard to have children. Specialist doctors found nothing physically wrong with them, and advised them to relax and be patient. I advised Mrs Ong to practise Hula-Hoop, in combination with Lifting the Sky and Carrying the Moon, followed by induced chi flow and meditation (to be discussed in Chapters 7 and 10). After three months she conceived. Then I told her to leave out Lifting the Sky, Carrying the Moon and induced chi flow, but carry on with Hula-Hoop (without any vigorous movements) and meditation. She delivered a healthy baby girl, followed by a boy a year later.

Deep Knee Bending

Hussein, aged 19, was afflicted by a disabling illness, the technical name of which I could neither pronounce nor remember. His left leg was very much thinner than his right. He could hardly walk or squat, and had been suffering for three years. His loving father brought him from Alor Setar to Sungai Petani three times a week to see me for chi kung therapy.

For the first few sessions I opened some of his vital points on his arms and body as well as his legs, and transmitted my chi into him. Vital points are spots on the body where a therapist can influence a patient's internal energy flow. They are the same as acu-points in acupuncture. A trained person can open vital points of another person by correctly and gently rubbing a finger on them. Later I taught him Lifting the Sky and Abdominal Breathing, which he did while sitting down. When he had gained more confidence and strength, he added Pushing Mountains and Hula-Hoop to his training programme, and he gradually performed most of the exercises standing, though a chair was always nearby for him to sit on if he needed to.

After about four months he could stand long enough to perform induced chi flow. Meanwhile we were greatly encouraged that his thin left leg was growing bigger and stronger. Two months later I taught him Deep Knee Bending, which proved to be the most difficult yet most important exercise for him, and which he initially practised with the help of railings. The muscles around his knee had become so stiff that he could hardly bend his legs. But Hussein was a brave and determined boy. Despite numerous tumbles resulting in good-hearted laughs which he himself joined in (but, of course, no one ever ridiculed him for his handicap), he persevered. After about three months of hard work, he could bend and walk reasonably well. His left leg was still slightly smaller than his right, but he proudly told me that he could now ride the motor-cycle his father had promised him as a reward.

From the ready position, raise your arms forward to shoulder level so that your fingers point in front. At the same time, raise your heels to stand on your toes, and breathe in gently, Figure 5.3(a). Visualize cosmic energy flowing into you. Use abdominal breathing if you can; if not, breathe in your normal way.

Keeping your balance on your toes and holding your arms in front at shoulder level, squat down fully, or as low as you can, breathing out in the process and visualizing energy flowing up your spine from your huiyin vital point near the anus to the baihui vital point at the crown of your head, Figure 5.3(b).

Next, still on your toes and with your arms in front, raise your body to the starting position, Figure 5.3(c). Simultaneously breathe in and visualize energy flowing down the front of your body from your head to your abdomen.

Then gracefully lower your arms and your heels to the normal standing position, which is also the ready position, with your open palms facing backward, Figure 5.3(d). At the same time breathe out and visualize energy flowing to your fingers and toes. Repeat the procedure a suitable number of times.

Fig 5.3(a), (b), (c)   Deep Knee Bending

This is an excellent exercise to stimulate chi flow to the hands and feet. It is effective for relieving rheumatism, arthritis and internal injuries. For advanced students, it helps to attain the breakthrough of the 'small universe' and the 'big universe', which are remarkable chi kung achievements whereby chi flows harmoniously through the conceptual and governing meridians, and the 12 main meridians respectively (*see* Chapter 9).

Circulating Knees

Although Circulating Knees is a very simple exercise, it has some useful specific functions. It loosens our knees after standing still for some time, and it stimulates chi to flow in a circular manner. Hence, it is often used as the last of a series of dynamic chi kung exercises, or after quiescent chi kung such as Abdominal Breathing and Standing Meditation. It is also frequently used to induce circular chi flow inside our body, a fascinating, incredible exercise which will be explained in Chapter 7.

Mrs Loh, aged 56, had suffered from arthritis for many years, and her knees were often swollen. Sometimes the pain was so severe and crippling that she literally had to drag herself up her stairs. Circulating Knees was one of the many exercises that helped her to recover so satisfactorily that she gratefully told her friends the chi kung course she took from me was worth more than a thousand times the fee she paid.

Rub your palms together to warm them and place them on your knees. Next, with your palms still on your knees, rotate your knees about ten time to one side, Figure 5.4, then rotate them about the same number of times to the other side. Breathe naturally. Then stand upright, close your eyes, relax and enjoy chi massaging your knees.

Fig 5.4   Circulating Knees

Convenient Classification of Chi Kung

All the ten chi kung exercises described in this chapter and the previous two chapters fall into a category of chi kung known as dynamic chi kung. While there are literally hundreds of such dynamic chi kung exercises or patterns, these ten patterns are among the best, and as such, they are found in many other styles of chi kung beside Shaolin Chi Kung, the style presented in this book.

These exercises are called dynamic because they involve visible movements. Thus, they are sometimes called external chi kung. Dynamic or external chi kung is a good contrast to quiescent chi kung, which is sometimes referred to as internal chi kung. Some examples of quiescent chi kung are Abdominal Breathing (Chapter 9) and Standing and Sitting Meditation (Chapter 10), though meditation may sometimes be classified in a separate category.

These terms, 'dynamic' and 'quiescent', 'external' and 'internal', are only convenient, often arbitrary, descriptions; and should not be taken as rigid designations. All chi kung, including dynamic chi kung or external chi kung, is fundamentally internal, and any students who concentrate mainly on its dynamic and external features will miss its essence. On the other hand, don't be misled by the term 'quiescent', thinking that it is soft or passive. Generally, quiescent chi kung is more advanced than dynamic chi kung, and is more powerful.

Sometimes it may not be easy to describe a particular kind of chi kung, like self-manifested chi movement (or induced chi flow), as dynamic or quiescent because it involves both mobile and stationary aspects. Actually, all kinds of chi kung have both dynamic and quiescent features; it is usually a matter of which group of features is more prominent or obvious that determines the classification of that particular chi kung type into its dynamic or quiescent category. For example, there are also quiescent features, such as standing still and clearing all thoughts, in dynamic chi kung; and there are dynamic features, such as internal energy flow and active visualization, in quiescent chi kung.

In self-manifested chi movement, the dynamic and the quiescent features are almost equally significant. Therefore, many chi kung masters refer to self-manifested chi movement as a separate category, known by the rather prosaic though practical term dynamic-quiescent chi kung.

Some readers, not yet familiar with chi kung terminology, may find these concepts – like 'quiescent chi kung can be dynamic and more powerful', 'external chi kung is basically internal' – rather puzzling. One major cause of such difficulty is the linguistic and cultural difference between Chinese and English. Nevertheless, if we bear in mind that these terms are for convenience and often arbitrary, we can reduce much of this difficulty and gain a better appreciation of this fascinating art.

6

WOULD YOU LIKE TO MAXIMIZE RESULTS?

Useful Advice for Chi Kung Training

❖ *If you want good health and vitality, you must not merely read about them, but must practise the proper techniques to acquire them.*

Maximum Results in Minimum Time

I am proud that my chi kung school, Shaolin Wahnam Chi Kung Institute, charges one of the highest fees in the region, yet we have one of the largest numbers of students. One important reason for our success is that we help our students to set aims and objectives, then help them to fulfill them. Another reason is that we show our students how to obtain maximum results in minimum time. We believe that if a student can accomplish his objectives in six months, we will not take a year to teach him. Therefore, the seemingly high fees turn out to be most economical.

How do we maximize results? Our approaches are summarized in our 'Ten Do's and Don'ts' and 'Right Habits'. They are actually not our invention; we merely gathered some of the best advice past masters had passed down to us, and put it together into some convenient systems.

The Ten Do's in Chi Kung Training

- The first and foremost 'do' – without which all wonderful knowledge and expert instruction, and all the other advice, become useless – is to practise regularly and consistently. Chi kung is not a subject like history or biology which you can read up on and become knowledgeable. It is an art which necessitates a lot of practice. If you want good health and vitality, you must not merely read about them, but must practise the proper techniques to acquire them.

- As far as possible, practise in natural surroundings where the air is fresh and circulating. If you remember that chi kung is not a system of physical exercise where you train bones and muscles, but an internal discipline where the main ingredient is cosmic energy that is manifested as fresh air to most people, you can better appreciate the importance of natural surroundings. However, if the weather is not favourable, you may practise indoors, provided that the air is not stale.

- The best time to practise is at sunrise, which chi kung masters refer to as the time of creative energy. Another excellent time is at midnight, which is the time of blossoming energy. Other suitable times are between seven and nine in the morning, and between five and ten in the evening.

- Better results are obtained if you practise facing the east. Some masters and some authoritative chi kung literature (from the northern hemisphere) recommend facing the south. By implication, if you are in the southern hemisphere, it would be best to face the north. Facing an open sea or an open space is also a good direction. These directions are ideal, that is, to be followed if it is feasible; it does not means that facing other directions is detrimental.

- You must be relaxed and cheerful during your training. The mind is the most important element of chi kung. Much of the benefit derived from chi kung is from the mental aspect, not from the outward form nor even the breath control. A relaxed and cheerful attitude enables you to get the best from your mental aspect.

- One direct method to use your mind rewardingly in chi kung training is to think gently of cosmic energy flowing into you, cleansing you of illness and toxic waste, and giving you radiant health and vitality. However, you must operate this mental aspect gently. It is a mistake to think that all this is mere imagination. Those with psychic sight, can see the flow of cosmic energy.

- It is helpful to drink some warm water or other warm

beverage before training to facilitate sweating. Sweating is one of the major ways, especially at the beginners' stage, to clear toxic waste from your body. Later, as you progress in your development, you may sweat less. So, if you find that you are not sweating as much as you did when you started chi kung, it is not that you are getting poorer results; it probably means that you have cleared away much of the rubbish that needs to be cleared, and are now ready for a new phase where developing (rather than cleansing) energy is more significant.

- Wear loose clothing and flat-bottomed shoes to facilitate chi flow in your body. Loosen your belt and collar. Take off your watch, rings and bracelets if they interfere with chi flow.

- Perform your breathing and movement gently, gracefully and naturally. In chi kung training the most important ingredient that you breathe in is not air but cosmic energy. Gentle, graceful breathing and movement facilitates smooth flow of cosmic energy.

- Be kind and generous in your dealings with all people. This advice has been given by many great chi kung masters in history. The reason is not just altruism: because our universe is intricately and organically interconnected, being kind and generous to others will result in being kind and generous to yourself.

The Ten Don'ts in Chi Kung Training

- Don't stop or interrupt your daily practice – this is the most common cause of students failing to attain good results. If you practise off and on, you will not get good results even if you practise for a long time, for you will miss the essential cumulative effect of chi kung training. When you think you are too busy, or feel you are too lazy, even a few minutes of practice will help to maintain your progress. If you realize that none of the many things that make you busy every day is more important than your health, you will be better inspired to practise your daily chi kung. However, if you have to miss your practice once in a while, it is all right so long as your overall training is regular. On the other hand, don't over-practise until you become tired.

- Don't practise in crowded, noisy, smelly or dirty places, where the air is stale or polluted. The polluted air, or negative energy, that you take in will more than offset the little benefit you get from your physical movements, thus making the training more harmful than beneficial.
- Don't practise at noon, or when it is very hot. Past masters said that during such unfavourable times the cosmic energy was too 'forceful'. In modern scientific terms, it probably means that cosmic radiation is too strong and hence harmful to our cells.
- Don't practise near a cemetery, in a violently moving vehicle, or in lightning and thunderstorms. My master explained that the chi near a cemetery was too 'dead' or too yin. (Perhaps modern scientists may verify if the air around a cemetery is not favourable to life.) A violently moving vehicle may cause the chi in the student to flow astray, while the chi during lightning and thunderstorms is so powerfully charged that it is harmful to body cells.
- Don't practise when you are tense, irritated, furious, frightened or anxious. These negative emotions block energy flow and are harmful to the 'heart', which, in Chinese, often refers to the mind. Chi kung actually helps us to overcome these negative emotions (or negative energy), but if they are too overwhelming it is better to stop practising for the time being.
- If you have any problems on our mind, put them aside, at least for the few minutes of your chi kung practice. (After practice, if you still want your problems, you may take them back.) One useful way to drop your mental problems during practice, is to be gently mindful of what you are practising. Since you have only one mind, when that mind is fully (but gently) occupied with chi kung techniques there is no room for other thoughts, including problems which you had previously imagined to be important.
- Don't have a heavy meal or a cold bath immediately before or after your training; neither should you be hungry nor stuffily uncomfortable. A heavy meal interferes with chi flow, while water vapour may enter your body through pores in your skin which open up during chi kung practice.
- Don't wear tight clothing nor practise bare-footed. Tight clothing restricts physical movements as well as internal chi

flow. Negative energy from the ground may enter your feet if you are bare-footed. If you like wearing high-heeled shoes, wear them only after your chi kung practice.

- Don't use force in your breathing nor exert force in your chi kung movements. It is a common misconception among beginners to think that the more forcefully they breathe, the more force they will develop. What is breathed in is not just air, but cosmic energy, and forced breathing or forced movements constrict the flow of cosmic energy.

- Don't be mean or malicious in any of your dealings with any persons. In addition to the cosmic dimension of meanness and malice rebounding to the mean and malicious person because of the interconnectedness of the universe, at a more personal level the negative energy generated when a person becomes mean or malicious is harmful to himself.

Right Habits for Best Results

As well as the 'do's' and 'don'ts', there are other factors that affect the rate of progress and level of attainment, and they are incorporated in the 'Song of Right Habits in Chi Kung Training' as follows:

> United as one are the elements three
> And the three hearts firm and strong
> The posture upright and proper be
> The breathing gentle, deep and long
> The mind is focused, clear and fresh
> Relaxed, calm and natural we maintain
> Sure and gradual our progress and quest
> Externally and internally we must train
> With ourselves and the cosmos we are at peace
> Be humble in learning and diligent in practice

The three elements of chi kung are form, breathing and mind, and you must achieve a harmonious co-ordination of these elements in your training. In other words, the dynamic movements or the static posture, the various breath controls, and the appropriate gentle visualization must be performed as one unity. For example, if you just perform the physical movements without the supportive breathing, or merely breathe in and out without the proper mental guidance, then you will not achieve the best results.

The three hearts here refer to the heart of confidence, the heart of patience and the heart of perseverance. You must have confidence that your instructor is competent and your method is effective. If you lack this confidence you have to find another instructor or method. You need patience. Even a simple flower takes a few months to bear fruit; you should give yourself at least a few months to see results. You must persevere to deserve reward. The advice that 'nothing worthwhile is ever obtained without effort' serves as good motivation.

The form of your chi kung training, that is, the various movements in dynamic chi kung or the poise in quiescent chi kung, must be correct. Although form is the least important element in chi kung, practising the form correctly enables you to draw out the most that form is designed to give. On the other hand, you should not be unduly worried over the exactness of your form. There is always allowance for individual difference and weakness.

Your breathing, the second element of chi kung, should be slow, deep and gentle. Never, ever, force your breathing. Breathing forcefully often leads to undesirable side effects, like giddiness and chest pain. Breathing out is as important as breathing in; in fact at the elementary stage breathing out is more important. A pause, but not a direct break, at various appropriate places in the breathing process, is also significant; but you must not hold the pause forcefully. If, while pausing, you feel your breath wanting to come in or out, let that wonderful stream of life flow its natural course.

Your mind, the third element of chi kung, must be handled with care and gentleness; it is not that it is brittle or fragile, but forced handling will create stress which is very harmful. The mind, as William James, the father of American psychology, said, is 'the most powerful force in the world'; using gentle visualization to achieve good chi kung results is only a very small expression of its capability.

To provide the best environment for your mind to function, and also for your chi to flow harmoniously, you should remain relaxed, calm and natural, not only mentally but physically too. Tensing your muscles, for example, interrupts smooth energy flow; being anxious creates negative energy; and holding an unnatural pose (unless you are specially trained, like yogis) distracts mental concentration. By paying careful attention to this principle, you will not only enhance your results, but also do much to prevent possible deviations.

Your progress must be systematic and gradual. You must allow sufficient time for your body to adjust to the new energy level that you will attain during chi kung training. When a certain organ is diseased, for example, other healthy organs function in ways that support or compensate for the diseased organ. The recovery, therefore, must be gradual enough to allow other organs to adjust to the new healthy environment. Progress that is too rapid or haphazard can be harmful to the body.

Your training must be internally and externally co-ordinated. Although internal cultivation is the hallmark of chi kung, you must not neglect its physical, external aspects, such as the various muscle stretching and joint rotating movements in the dynamic chi kung patterns described in the three previous chapters. If you only cultivate internal aspects, like energy and mind, you may be healthy and mentally fresh, even spiritually advanced, but your muscles may be so tight and your joints so stiff that you can hardly turn your body.

Your daily life should be normal and appropriate. A person, for example, may be practising an effective chi kung exercise to cure a particular disease, but if he still exposes himself to the negative factors that contributed to his disease, like late nights, heavy smoking or irritability, the benefits that he derives from chi kung may be offset by his continual negative conduct.

You must be humble and ready in your learning, and regular and diligent in your practice. It is amazing how many people, perhaps attempting to cover their weakness, keep aloof from seeking knowledge or even disregard knowledge that is offered to them, and adopt an attitude suggesting that their style or methods are the best. This attitude must have been common since ancient times, for past masters frequently advised that we should be humble in our quest for knowledge. But even if we are knowledgeable, we must practise regularly and diligently.

By following such advice to maximize results in minimum time, you will be better prepared to learn and practise more chi kung exercises. In the next chapter you will be introduced to a fantastic type of chi kung that you may not believe to be possible. Here is a good opportunity to test credibility against validity, to test whether the incredible things written in some chi kung literature are really true. The benefit, of course, is not just to satisfy your curiosity; the chi kung exercises that you are going to read about, and hopefully practise, are among the best for promoting health and vitality.

7

THE FASCINATION OF ENERGY FLOWING IN YOU

Benefits and Techniques of Self-Manifested
Movement

❖ *The Shaolin Wahnam Self-Manifested Chi
Movement exercises presented here provide a useful
method for experiencing chi as well as directing chi
flow.*

A Fascinating, Incredible Art

Would you believe that certain types of chi kung could make
you sway or move about involuntarily, dance about gracefully,
perform kungfu movements even though you have not learnt
kungfu, or even roar like a tiger or gambol like a deer with your
fingers forming the deer's antlers? I didn't believe it – not until I
saw and experienced it myself.

This chapter provides an opportunity for you to experience
this kind of chi kung, and you will find the practice both
enjoyable and beneficial. It is a very useful method to cleanse the
body of illness and toxic waste, and to generate harmonious
energy flow.

This kind of chi kung is called self-manifested chi movement
or induced chi flow, which is 'zi fa dong gong' in Chinese,
meaning 'the art of self-manifested movements'. Those not
familiar with Romanized Chinese pronunciation may like to
know that 'dong gong' is pronounced like 'tung kung'.

Some people may have practised chi kung for many years, yet
have no experience of what chi, or life energy, is. Others do not
believe that a person can really direct chi to whichever part of

the body he wishes. The Shaolin Wahnam Self-Manifested Chi Movement exercises presented here provide a useful method for experiencing chi as well as directing chi flow.

Actually, chi flows inside all of us. Like blood flow, it is so normal that most people are not aware of it. In a self-manifested movement or induced chi flow exercise, especially when a master has helped the student to open up some vital points, the rate and the volume of chi flow are greatly increased. Hence, the student can experience chi flow; often it is manifested outwardly as involuntary swaying or gentle movements. Sometimes the practitioner moves out from his position and performs some dance-like or kungfu motions. Occasionally the movements can be vigorous, and the practitioner may shout or hit himself (and enjoy it) or roll on the ground!

There is absolutely nothing occult, spiritualistic or religious in self-manifested chi movement. The involuntary movements are caused by chi moving in the body, which is perfectly natural, and not by any outside force. Chi is flowing in our body all the time; in this exercise we enhance its flow. It does not interfere at all with any religious beliefs, and, therefore, can be practised by people of any religion.

The person doing induced chi flow is not in a trance; he is perfectly aware of his actions and surroundings. He is in control – a very important aspect in this category of chi kung exercises – and can stop his movements if he wishes. He carries on his funny movements, if any, because he likes doing so and knows that it is beneficial to him. These extraordinary actions, however, are not common; usually he sways gracefully.

Enjoying Self-Manifested Movement

Let us now enjoy this fascinating self-manifested movement exercise. Most students find the experience memorable and gratifying.

Stand upright and relaxed. For men, use the left middle finger to press gently on the navel about ten times. For women, use the right middle finger. (However, in your practice if you get mixed up with left and right, do not be unduly worried.) This pressing with your finger is to stimulate your chi at your abdominal energy field. Then place the other middle finger on the crown of your head and massage in a rotary manner about three times. This is to open the baihui (meaning 'the meeting of hundred meridians') vital point, and acts as a safety valve for excessive energy to flow over instead of being blocked at the head.

Then perform Lifting the Sky (p 22) about ten to fifteen times. After each time, pause (but do not completely stop) for one or two seconds to visualize energy flowing down your body from your head to your feet.

After repeating Lifting the Sky ten or fifteen times, continue with Pushing Mountains (p 30) for another ten to fifteen times. Feel the flow of energy to your arms and legs, or any other parts of your body. Continue with Carrying the Moon (p 32), also for ten to fifteen times, visualizing a waterfall of wonderful energy cascading down your body. After each time, pause (but do not completely stop) for a second or two to feel this internal shower.

Then stand fairly still and close your eyes. If you feel that chi is moving you, follow its momentum and enjoy the self-manifested movements. If you are not yet moving substantially, visualize chi flowing down from your head through your body to your feet. Gently visualize this three or four times. Next, think of your nose once, and then think of your feet. Then let go of yourself completely, as if drifting in the clouds.

If you have done the above correctly, and are relaxed sufficiently, your chi will now be flowing inside your body, and you will be swaying pleasantly. However, some people may not move much, though chi is flowing inside, while others may move vigorously. A few may dance or run about, or even shout, laugh or cry. All these are normal reactions, and are beneficial to the student. But if you are practising on your own, you should not allow your movements to be too vigorous. This can be controlled quite easily: as you begin to move vigorously, just tell yourself to go slow. It is as simple as that!

Close your eyes and be totally relaxed while enjoying chi flow in your body. It is a form of flowing meditation. Later, when you are quite advanced in this art, you may open your eyes if you like. During the sway of the chi flow you may, if you wish, gently think of your illness or injured parts. This will direct chi to flow to your illness or injury to treat it. This is directed induced chi flow.

If you have no particular illness, just savour the very pleasant sensation of chi flow balancing the energy levels in your body. This is free induced chi flow. Even if you want to cure a known disease, it is advisable to have free chi flow sometimes, instead of only directed chi flow targeted at the disease, because free chi flow allows energy to cure insidious illness that you yourself may not know of but which is developing inside you. This is one of the ways in which chi kung prevents illness.

After about ten minutes of self-manifested movements, or when you have enjoyed enough of the chi flow, gently tell your movements to slow down. You will be surprised at how well your mind can control your movements. Concentrate your chi at your abdomen, and gracefully bring your movements to a gentle stop. Stand still for a few seconds, and gently think of your abdomen – this will focus your energy there, helping you to be 'grounded'. Rub your palms together, place them on your eyes, and dab your eyes with your palms as open your eyes. Then walk about briskly.

Different people may react differently because of their different constitutions and other factors. Some move vigorously, others may hardly move at all. So, if you merely feel energy tingling in your cells while your friends are swaying like willow trees, this does not necessarily mean you are getting less benefit. On the other hand, if you find yourself hitting various parts of your body and you enjoy doing that, don't worry, you are not becoming sadistic; this self-hitting is one remarkable way chi kung cures your sickness. Your vital energy, as manifested in induced chi flow, knows your needs better than the conscious you does! In the meditative state of induced chi flow, if you let nature lead the way while you do 'nothing', your vital energy will operate in the best possible way for your needs.

The Circular Flow

There are five major steps in the methodology of self-manifested chi movement.

1 Stimulate innate energy at the navel and open the 'safety valve' at the crown of the head.
2 Perform chi kung patterns that induce internal energy flow. (If energy is flowing sufficiently to move the body 'involuntarily', skip step 3 and proceed to step 4 below.)
3 Visualize energy flowing down from head to feet.
4 Relax totally and enjoy the poetic motion of the self-manifested movement induced by internal energy flow. This forms the main part of the exercise.
5 Gradually slow down and stop gracefully.

In step 2 above, we can use other chi kung patterns instead of the three patterns described earlier, and we need not stick to three patterns nor to ten to fifteen times per pattern. Some people may have to perform more patterns, or perform each pattern more times, to start the self-manifested chi movements. Advanced practitioners need to perform just one pattern – Carrying the Moon would be a good choice in this case – a few times to start the internal energy moving. Some masters do not even have to perform any pattern; they can readily induce chi flow by just using their mind.

The choice of patterns will influence the way a practitioner moves in his self-manifested movements. The example we used – Lifting the Sky, Pushing Mountains and Carrying the Moon – is an excellent choice, because the self-manifested movements generated are poetic, and the induced internal energy flow is holistic.

On the other hand, if we wish to have a different kind of manifested movement during an induced chi flow exercise, we can choose different kind of patterns to induce the movements. For example, if we desire to have circular movements, we can choose patterns that tend to induce circular movements, such as Circulating Head, Merry-Go-Round and Hula-Hoop. However, while the resultant movements are likely to be circular, it is not a certainty. Because of our bodily needs and other factors, our resultant movements may sometimes be different from the ones our chosen patterns are intended to cause.

Perhaps you may like to try self-manifested movement using the 'circular patterns'. The procedure is the same, and is as follows.

> Gently press on your navel about ten times with a left finger for men, or right for women. Then use a finger of the other hand to massage the crown of your head about three times.
>
> Perform Circulating Head (p 34) (just the rotating movement will do) about three to five times each side in this case, not ten to fifteen times. Then perform Merry-Go-Round (p 36), also three to five times each side. Continue with Hula-Hoop (p 41) about 20 to 30 times each side.
>
> Then keep fairly still and visualize chi flowing down the body. When your body starts to move, enjoy the self-manifested movement. Complete the exercise by willing yourself to a gentle stop.

This self-manifested chi movement is one of the best chi kung exercises for health and vitality, and it is really easy once you are familiar with its procedure. Although it has been practised since ancient times, it is not widely known because, in line with traditional practice, the best methods were kept secret from the populace. If you practise induced chi flow for 15 minutes daily, you must be prepared to forfeit the chance to see your doctor again in his professional capacity!

Some Essential Points to Bear in Mind

Another reason why such an excellent chi kung technique was not widely practised was because people were scared of stumbling and hurting themselves. This fear was magnified because in the past many chi kung instructors strove to mystify this art instead of explaining it. It was (and still is) easy for a selfish instructor to mislead his students by encouraging them to imagine that they had developed some serious deviation when they started to move involuntarily. A selfish chi kung therapist might tell his clients that such self-manifested movements, though effective for curing illness, have to be initiated by the therapist himself (and for a handsome fee), when it is actually easier for the clients to practise on their own.

Of course there are pitfalls in induced chi flow, and in all other types of chi kung, just as there are in many of the other paths we have to travel along. But if we are informed about the pitfalls beforehand so that we can avoid them, our journey will be safe. Our safety will be doubly assured if we also know how to get out from the pitfalls should we, despite prior warning, stumble into them. This getting out, the remedial exercises to correct deviations, will be explained in Chapter 11 for your information even though you may never have to use it. Meanwhile, we shall examine the pitfalls of self-manifested chi movement.

It is very important not to go against the momentum of the chi flow inside your body. If you abruptly stop your body from moving, or purposely go against the flowing momentum, while your vital energy is still flowing strongly, the energy may hit you inside, making you uncomfortable and possibly causing injury.

If you have a qualified instructor supervising you, you can simply let go and let your internal chi flow dictate your movements even if they become vigorous. You may experience a tiger's roar or a kangaroo's hop even during the first few practices. But if you train on your own, you must release control gradually, allowing the tiger's roar, kangaroo's hop or other vigorous and interesting movements to occur only when you are sure of your ability.

Initially, allow yourself to move on your own only slightly. Then allow more and more movement, until eventually – when you are sure your conscious control can take over whenever you desire – you can completely release your control and allow your chi to move you however it will. It is like learning to swim in an open sea, except that self-manifested chi movement is many times safer. First you stay near the waterline, then you inch farther out, making sure that the water only reaches your waist. Later you move to chest level, and only when you are completely sure of your swimming skills, do you venture out to the sea.

If your movements become too vigorous, gently tell yourself to slow down. On rare occasions, the momentum of your internal energy flow may speed up so much that you may not be ready to control it. This rarely happens unless the volume of vital energy in you is already tremendous and your pathways of energy flow are fairly clear. But even if this happens, do not panic. Follow the fast momentum, breathe in and out slowly, and simultaneously assure yourself that you are in control. Then slowly and firmly tell your movements to slow down. It is that simple! Your mind can control your movements – this is a natural law. When you appear to move without your volition it is because your mind allows it so.

If you are in a deep meditative mood while enjoying the self-manifested movements and there is a sudden disturbance, such as a loud sound, tell yourself that the disturbance cannot harm you, and think of your energy and mind being intact. This is a very important point that will prevent possible side-effects.

Make sure that the place where you perform the self-manifested chi movement is safe; for example, it should not be near a balcony or sharp objects. No one should disturb you while you are in the midst of your induced chi flow. If someone approaches you, indicate to him to wait while you get ready to stop the exercise. If your telephone rings, do not answer it immediately. By the time you stop the exercise, the telephone may have stopped ringing, but if the call is sufficiently important the caller will call again.

When you wish to complete the exercise, do not stop abruptly, especially when your movements are still vigorous. By using your mind to will it, you can gradually slow down your movements, then bring yourself to a graceful stop. Remember to stand for at least a few seconds 'to bring your energy home' to your abdomen before walking away.

A good book, at its best, is only a poor substitute for a master. If, after reading this book, you feel inspired to practise chi kung, seek a good master so that you can get the best for your health and vitality.

8

CHI KUNG IS NOT JUST A GENTLE DANCE

Important Aspects of Chi Kung

❖ *When we understand the three elements of chi kung, it becomes obvious that if we just practise chi kung form, as many students do, even at best we can only attain a small portion of what chi kung can offer us.*

More Than What We See

The movements of dynamic chi kung and self-manifested chi movement are always graceful and rhythmic, appropriately described as poetry in motion. But we would be grossly mistaken to think chi kung is some sort of gentle dance. Firstly, the dance-like movements are only one aspect of chi kung – in many ways the least important aspect. Secondly, there are other types of chi kung that are not dance-like, though they are also generally gentle and rhythmic.

In fact, one major reason why many students do not progress very far in chi kung though they may have practised for a long time, is their misguided emphasis on this dance-like aspect only, their neglect of the other less obvious but more important aspects, and their ignorance of other types of chi kung in which this dance-like aspect is not prominent. The dance-like aspect constitutes the form of chi kung. There are literally hundreds of different kinds of chi kung, but all chi kung consists of three aspects or elements, namely form, energy and mind.

The Visible, External Element

Form is the visible, external aspect of chi kung, the element which we can see. For example, as described in previous chapters, when you perform Lifting the Sky, the way you stand and move your hands constitutes its form. When you perform self-manifested chi movement, all the postures and actions that can be clearly seen – from pressing on your navel and performing various physical exercises, to swaying gently or moving vigorously, and rubbing your palms to warm your eyes – are the form of chi kung. When you perform Abdominal Breathing (to be explained in Chapter 9), the manner in which you stand stationary holding your hand at your abdomen, apparently doing nothing else for ten to fifteen minutes, constitutes the form of this chi kung exercise.

Although form is the least important of the three elements of chi kung, it is still important. The form of the particular type of chi kung we practise – the way we pose and move our body – is the crystallization of hundreds of years of study and experimentation by past masters in their quest for health, vitality and personal development. In other words, when we learn a certain chi kung form from our instructor, this form is not his invention, but has been evolved and perfected throughout the ages to be bequeathed to us. Therefore, performing the form correctly enables us to derive the greatest benefits that form is designed to give. If we perform the form incorrectly, not only may we not get the greatest benefit, but we may sometimes get undesirable side-effects instead.

What good advice can we follow to avoid practising the form incorrectly? First, an excellent guiding principle, handed down by generations of chi kung masters, is to perform chi kung forms gently, gracefully and naturally. Except for some 'hard chi kung' found in martial arts, it is of utmost importance not to force chi kung movements. This paradox of not using strength in chi kung, yet acquiring tremendous strength, has been a constant puzzle to the uninitiated, and a fascination to the adepts. Secondly, chi kung form must be graceful, not rigid or staccato.

The third requirement, that of being natural, needs some explanation. Of course, movements like Plucking Stars and standing stationary holding our abdomen are not actions we normally do in our daily life; these movements are actually 'unnatural' to those not trained in them. But they are 'natural' in promoting better energy flow or in enhancing energy levels; they correspond to nature's way of giving us health and vitality. All these three features of proper chi kung form – being gentle, graceful and natural – are meant to develop energy.

Tapping Cosmic Energy

Energy, or chi in Chinese, is the second element of chi kung. It is an invisible aspect, although those with psychic sight may see energy flow in a chi kung practice. There are many kinds of energy, but generally energy that is inside us is referred to as vital energy, and energy that is outside us as cosmic energy. Energy is the element that gives chi kung its name.

Energy is usually, but not always, expressed in breathing. Hence, some people refer to chi kung as the art of breathing, which is not correct. Breathing may be broadly divided into three parts: breathing out, breathing in and pause. These different parts may be arranged in a different order for specific purposes, and the time taken for each part may vary. The usual breathing process in chi kung is to breathe out slowly, pause for a short while, breathe in slowly, pause for a short while, and repeat. If we wish to conserve energy to carry out some forceful actions speedily, and not be exhausted at the completion of the actions, as in kungfu sparring, we may use the following procedure: breathe in fast, pause for a long time (while we perform the kungfu movements), breathe out gently.

Normally we breathe in through the nose and out through the mouth. But for some special effects, we may use different combinations. In performing a Tai Chi Chuan set, for example, some masters use the nose for both breathing in and out. Except in the case of some hard chi kung patterns, breathing must be done gently, gracefully and naturally. Forced breathing is often a cause of deviation.

Breathing is not the only technique chi kung practitioners use to tap energy. Some schools of chi kung teach their students to use their hands to tap energy from luxuriant plants or sturdy trees, but we from Shaolin Wahnam disagree with this methodology because we believe this will harm the plants. One of my disciples did an unforgettable experiment. He tapped energy from a resplendent plant. After three days of tapping, the plant almost dried up. My disciple quickly transmitted his own vital energy to the plant. A few days later the plant regained its resplendence.

Wilfully sucking energy from another person – through sexual intercourse, for instance – to nourish oneself is unethical. The person sucking out the energy may also take in any sickness (not necessarily venereal diseases) or other negative energy from that person. Such a mean practice is actually taught by some chi kung groups and religious sects. Why stoop to such a technique when we can readily tap free, abundant, wonderful cosmic energy from the open universe?

Some chi kung masters can tap cosmic energy with their whole body. Therefore, in some advanced chi kung exercises there is no need for conscious breath control. A master may go into deep meditation and let cosmic energy bathe his every cell! At such a level, the master attains, or at least approaches, spiritual fulfilment. This is possible when he has fully developed the third element of chi kung – mind.

Mind, the Most Important Element

Mind is the most important of the three chi kung elements. While the mind aspect is most significant at the advanced level – advanced chi kung is mainly if not wholly concerned with mind cultivation – it is also essential at the elementary stage, though many beginners may not be aware of this important point. Even when we are practising simple chi kung patterns for the basic purpose of maintaining physical well-being, if we only perform the form we will probably get less than 20 per cent of the potential benefits of that exercise. If we co-ordinate the form with correct breath control we may increase the benefit we get to 40 or 50 per cent of the potential. The greatest benefits can be obtained if we incorporate the element of mind; not just in wishful thinking, but in harmonizing mind, energy and form as one unity.

To attain such harmonious unity, our mind must first be still, for which there are two requirements: we should be physically and mentally relaxed, and our mind should be free from all irrelevant thoughts. To be able to relax physically and mentally is one of the first things we must learn in chi kung training. If we cannot do this, we are unlikely to progress very far in chi kung. When we are gently mindful of our hand and breathing movements while performing our chi kung patterns, we eliminate irrelevant thoughts. Probably without many of us realizing it, all the chi kung exercises we have learnt so far in this book help us to still our mind. We shall learn some other useful methods of mind cultivation in Chapter 10.

In some ways, the term 'chi kung' is a misnomer because the most important element is not chi or energy, but shen or mind. In fact, some great chi kung masters in China have suggested (and actually used) the term 'shengong', 'the art of developing mind', for advanced chi kung. However, the term 'chi kung' ('qigong' in Romanized Chinese) has caught on, as it has excellently served the function of referring to a wide range of arts that deal with energy (though energy may not be the most important element in some of these arts). Moreover, 'shengong' may have other unsuitable connotations.

When we understand the three elements of chi kung, it becomes obvious that if we just practise chi kung form, as many students do, even at best we can only attain a small portion of what chi kung can offer us. If you happen to be such a student, take consolation in the knowledge that this problem is prevalent, and can be readily remedied now that you have a better knowledge of chi kung. Chi kung masters have advised that to attain good results, one must have three harmonies. These three harmonies are 'the harmony of body', 'the harmony of breathing', and 'the harmony of mind'. The three harmonies are not separate, but are aspects of one unity.

Various Classifications of Chi Kung

The harmonious unity of form, energy and mind in chi kung can be accomplished in many different ways, resulting in countless different types of chi kung exercises, and numerous attempts have been made to classify them into convenient groups. One method is from their historical perspective, as described in Chapter 1, classifying chi kung into medical, martial, Confucianist, Taoist and Buddhist schools. Some masters group all other chi kung types that do not fall into these five major schools as populace chi kung.

Another classification is based on the posture the practitioner usually adopts in his chi kung training, namely standing, sitting, lying down and mobile chi kung. Another way is to divide chi kung into 'hard' and 'soft', or 'internal' and 'external', depending on the nature of training. It is interesting to note that hard chi kung can be internal, and soft chi kung external.

Chi kung is frequently divided into dynamic or quiescent, based on whether there are many visible movements in its training or none. There are two main kinds of dynamic chi kung, and also two main kinds of quiescent. Because these four main kinds are also discernably different within their own groups, it is useful to classify chi kung into four principal classes or approaches, namely dynamic chi kung, self-manifested chi movement, quiescent breathing, and meditation.

It must be remembered that all these classifications are for convenience; they are not rigid compartments. All the chi kung exercises described so far in this book can be classified as medical, standing, soft and dynamic. Nevertheless, some of the dynamic chi kung patterns, like Lifting the Sky and Pushing Mountains, are also found in martial art chi kung.

Four Fundamental Approaches

Dynamic chi kung is a generic term referring to the class of chi kung exercises where physical movements – either performed while the practitioner remains at the same spot or while he moves – can be clearly seen by others. It is developed from classical dao yin exercises, which were employed by the medical school of chi kung for curing illness, and by the Taoist school for promoting health and longevity. Dao yin means 'direct and lead'; dao yin and dynamic chi kung exercises are meant to direct and lead chi to flow harmoniously in the body. They are also useful exercises for stretching muscles and loosening joints.

The art of self-manifested movements, or induced chi flow, refers to the genre of chi kung exercises during which the practitioner moves about, sometimes gently, sometimes vigorously, occasionally making involuntary sounds, not of his own conscious doing. But the practitioner is in control, and is able to change or stop his movements if he wishes. It is excellent for cleansing meridians and harmonizing energy levels. Self-manifested chi movement has been practised since ancient times, but was kept exclusively for special people in the past. Han Wu Ti, the Martial Emperor of the Han Dynasty, lived to a ripe old age despite having 3,000 wives and pressing problems of an expanding empire because he practised self-manifested chi movement daily.

Quiescent breathing, the third genre of chi kung exercises, emphasizes breath control. The practitioner stands or sits still throughout the training, and onlookers may not notice any external movements, except perhaps the rise and fall of his abdomen or chest. The movements, however, are internal. By using various breathing methods and creative visualization, the practitioner can manipulate his internal energy flow in numerous interesting ways. He may, for example, send his vital energy to his liver to massage it, or circulate energy round his body to keep himself warm. We shall learn more about quiescent breathing in the next chapter.

Meditation, the fourth genre, is found in all schools of chi kung, be they medical, martial, Confucianist, Taoist or Buddhist. It can also be done in any posture – standing, sitting, lying down or moving – but standing and sitting meditation are most common. As meditation is chiefly concerned with mind cultivation, the most advanced stage of chi kung, many students may not have progressed to meditation by itself as a genre. In sitting meditation, the practitioner sits upright and apparently does nothing else for the whole training session. In reality, the meditator has two broad alternatives: he may keep his mind timelessly still, or he may go on a fascinating inward journey. We shall learn more about meditation in Chapter 10.

A holistic approach

Although all these chi kung approaches – dynamic chi kung, self-manifested chi movement, quiescent breathing, and medi-tation – are genres in their own right, it is best to have practised at least a bit of each approach if we want to have an ideal chi kung development. In the two more elementary genres – dynamic chi kung and self-manifested chi movement – breath control and mind cultivation are also introduced, though they are not trained to a very high level, and many students may have neglected them. But in the more advanced genres – quiescent breathing and meditation – the external aspects of chi kung that are characteristic of the other two genres, like gentle exercises and graceful movements, are not incorporated.

A suitable programme of chi kung training is to progress from the simple to the advanced, from dynamic chi kung and self-manifested chi movement to quiescent breathing and meditation. Problems may arise if a student proceeds to quiescent breathing or meditation directly. A student may develop much energy from quiescent breathing, but without the stretching and rotating exercises of dynamic chi kung and self-manifested chi movement, he may lack agility and ease of movement. He may have freshness of mind from meditation alone, but without the other chi kung elements he may lack energy or even be physically ill.

Not only do the different chi kung approaches enable us to develop holistically, the approaches also mutually enhance one another, so that our progress in any one chosen area will be faster as well as deeper. Breathing co-ordination and a meditative state of mind will greatly increase the benefits we gain, even if we want to specialize in dynamic chi kung or self-manifested chi movement.

In return, the gentle physical exercises of dynamic chi kung and self-manifested chi movement galvanize muscles and tendons so that the internal energy flow of quiescent breathing becomes smoother and stronger. The energy flow of self-manifested chi movement and quiescent breathing greatly helps meditation by cleansing brain cells of toxic waste and strengthening psychic centres. Some of my students had previously practised religious meditation for many years without much result. But after six months of drinking cosmic energy, a few acquired psychic abilities and all reported that they felt spiritually uplifted. If you want to drink cosmic energy too, turn to the next chapter.

9

TAKE A DRINK OF COSMIC ENERGY

The Why and How of Abdominal Breathing

❖ *When chi kung masters, while teaching Abdominal Breathing, say that they return to childhood, it is not just poetic fancy.*

The Secret of the Energy Masters

What do sportsmen, singers, yogi adepts, kungfu masters and children have in common? They all have abundant energy and they derive their energy from abdominal breathing. Children have abundant energy? Yes. Unless you are an athlete or trained in some special ways related to energy, I would bet my last dollar that if you play with a child, you will be tired after running around for ten minutes while that tiny tot is still bouncing with energy.

A child, still untainted by the habits learnt by adults, breathes naturally. Ask a child to lie flat, and observe how he breathes. You can easily see the rhythmic rise and fall of his abdomen as he takes in cosmic energy. Chi kung masters refer to abdominal breathing as natural breathing, and chest breathing as reversed breathing. Abdominal breathing is taught by nature, chest breathing is learnt by man. This can easily be verified if we compare the breathing of new-born babies, fresh from nature, and adults, exposed to the world.

As breath control is an essential element of chi kung, chi kung masters throughout the ages have experimented with and discovered many admirable breathing methods. Some of the more important ones are Abdominal Breathing, Reversed

Breathing, Cosmos Breathing, Foetus Breathing, Tortoise Breathing, Heel Breathing, Small Universe Breathing, Big Universe Breathing and No Breathing. Each technique has its special features and purposes, and the following description is only a very brief one.

Abdominal Breathing is the most fundamental of chi kung breathing. Cosmic energy is tapped and stored at the qihai (meaning 'the sea of energy') vital point at the abdomen. This breathing technique is very useful when we need much energy spread over a long period.

When explosive force is needed for a short time, for example, when executing a powerful punch or making the final dash in a running race, Reversed Breathing may be used. Cosmos Breathing employs chest breathing to tap cosmic energy from the universe and then store it in the abdomen. Foetus Breathing, reminiscent of the foetus in the mother's womb, is used for prolonged passivity where normal nose and mouth breathing is suspended and cosmic energy permeates in. If you wish to live as long as the tortoise, one of the revered divine creatures in Chinese philosophy, you may like to try Tortoise Breathing which is the art of breathing slowly and deeply as a tortoise does. In Heel Breathing, used by many illustrious Confucian scholars, you can breathe in cosmic energy right down to your heels – if you know the technique.

Small Universe Breathing, with chi continuously flowing round the ren and du meridians (to be explained later, see p 82), is much prized by kungfu masters, for it provides them with an endless supply of energy. It is also called microcosmic flow. Big Universe Breathing, or macrocosmic flow, with chi flowing through all the 12 primary meridians and permeating throughout the body, is employed by Taoist masters in their training to actualize immortality. No Breathing is breathing without conscious effort, where vital energy in the body merges with the cosmic energy of the universe, and is practised by Chan (Zen) masters to attain enlightenment.

It is illuminating to note that the more exact rendering of the term 'breathing' from Chinese to English is 'taking in cosmic energy', not 'taking in air', though many modern Chinese themselves may not be aware of it. The ancient Chinese had talked about breathing in chi, or energy, long before modern scientists knew about air. This also explains how chi can be breathed into the abdomen or any part of the body, while air is necessarily breathed into the lungs.

Returning to Childhood

When chi kung masters, while teaching Abdominal Breathing, say that they return to childhood, it is not just poetic fancy. When we practise Abdominal Breathing, not only do we breathe the way we did when we were children, we may also experience childhood sensations and rejuvenated functions. ('Abdominal Breathing', in capital letters, is used to refer to a special chi kung method of breathing, while 'abdominal breathing', in small letters, refers to using the abdomen in breathing.)

A few years ago I shared a memorable experience of returning to childhood with Dr Tan, who has the rare qualification of being trained in both Western and Chinese medicine. He was fascinated by chi kung, and begged me to accept him not just as a student but as a disciple. He suffered from hypertension, which he developed during his university days and which he knew could not be cured by conventional medicine. He had read that chi kung could cure it.

One night, after he had practised some dynamic chi kung patterns, I taught Dr Tan the first stage of Abdominal Breathing. The pressing and releasing of his abdomen at this stage led him into a meditative state of mind as he proceeded to Standing Meditation. Soon he bent backward involuntarily, and later his upper body began to sway in a circular manner. The graceful, circular swaying continued for about 15 minutes, during which we could see an expression of joy on his face.

As soon as he completed his chi kung exercise, he told me, 'Sifu, I just had a most wonderful experience. I returned to childhood!' 'How was it?' 'I felt I was a child. I really did. I felt my anterior fontanelle was opening.' Realizing that I might not be familiar with the Western medical term, he explained that was at the crown of the head where the baihui vital point was.

Soon his hypertension disappeared and it has never returned. All this happened within two weeks! This was my record for the fastest chi kung cure for hypertension; normally it would take about six months.

Don't Use Your Chest, Use Your Abdomen!

If you wish to return to childhood yet also wish to have a lot of energy to carry on with those adult activities you like, practise Abdominal Breathing. For those who have been used to chest breathing, changing to abdominal breathing is a difficult task if they do not know the training procedure. Many years ago, when I practised Wuzu Kungfu with a well-known master, I found that my senior classmates were full of internal power. ('Wuzu' is pronounced 'Goh Chor' in the Fujian dialect – the dialect commonly used by exponents of this Chinese martial art.)

My seniors told me that I must use abdominal breathing before I could train internal power. However, neither they nor my instructor taught me how to go about it systematically, though my instructor often reminded me to use abdominal breathing. 'How?' I asked. 'Don't use your chest to breathe; use your abdomen,' my instructor explained. I tried, and tried, but still could not succeed. I asked my seniors, and they replied, 'Don't use your chest to breathe, use your abdomen'. But after trying for more than a year I still could not breathe with my abdomen.

In this respect, you are luckier, for you will be able to perform abdominal breathing within two months if you follow the systematic steps below.

Stage 1

Stand with your feet fairly close together. Relax and empty your mind of all thoughts. Feel cheerful; smile from your heart. Place one palm (either one, though some masters recommend left for men and right for women) gently on top of your 'qihai' vital point, which is about three inches below your navel. Place the other palm on top of this palm. *See* Figure 9.1. You may perform the whole exercise with your eyes closed or open, or sometimes closed and sometimes open. Open your mouth slightly; your lips should be wide, not rounded.

Gently press on your abdomen with both palms for six counts. Your abdomen will fall. The pressing movement must be smooth and continuous, not staccato. Hold on for two counts. Then gently release your palms for six counts.

Fig 9.1 Pose for Abdominal Breathing

The releasing movement must be smooth and continuous, not staccato. Your abdomen will rise. Hold on for about two counts.

The whole process – pressing, holding, releasing, holding – constitutes one breathing unit, or one breath, although there should be no conscious attempt at breathing at this stage. Forget about your breathing – it will take care of itself. But it is important, very important, *not* to breathe in as you press on your abdomen. This breathing in as the chest rises is a very common mistake; and if you make this mistake, it is difficult to achieve abdominal breathing. One good way to avoid or overcome this mistake is to make an effort to forget your breathing. Gently focus your mind on the mechanical pressing and releasing of your palms, or on the mechanical falling and rising of your abdomen.

Repeat the process about ten times, that is, ten breathing units. Then drop your arms to your sides, with your palms facing the back, for Standing Meditation, Figure 9.2. Close your eyes (if they are not already closed) and forget about everything. If you have gently focused on your earlier palm movements or your rising and falling abdomen, you will by now have attained a pleasant chi kung state of mind.

Enjoy this state of nothingness for about five minutes, or what you think is five minutes. Then, still with your eyes closed, rub your palms together, place the centres of your

Fig 9.2   Standing Meditation

warm palms on your eyes and dab your eyes as you open
them. This constitutes the first stage of the Abdominal
Breathing exercise.

Practise this stage twice a day, once in the morning and
once in the evening or at night, for at least two weeks.
Gradually increase the number of breathing units as you
progress, but remember there should be no conscious
attempt at breathing at this stage. The six counts for
pressing and for releasing, and the two counts for holding,
are guidelines; you may gradually lengthen them if you feel
competent and comfortable. Only when you can perform
the falling and rising of your abdomen mechanically,
should you proceed to stage 2.

Stage 2

The next stage is similar to stage 1, except that as you press
on your abdomen, visualize or think of negative energy
flowing out from your abdomen up the front part of your
body and out through your mouth. Negative energy may
be translated as toxic waste, negative emotions, illness or
whatever you do not want. In other words, you press out all
the rubbish from your abdomen and other parts of your
body. Then, as your abdomen rises, visualize good cosmic
energy flowing through your nose, down the front part of

your body into your abdomen. This visualization must be gentle, and must never be overdone. If you find it too daunting, you need not visualize every time you press or release; a few times may be sufficient to set the outflow of rubbish and the inflow of cosmic energy in operation. There should still be no conscious attempt at breathing at this stage. Practise daily for at least two weeks before proceeding to the next stage.

Stage 3

Conscious breath control is introduced at stage 3. Perform the same procedure as at stage 2, except that as you press on the abdomen and visualize rubbish flowing out, gently breathe out through your mouth. As you release and visualize cosmic energy flowing in, gently breathe in through your nose. Your breathing must be gentle and graceful. Past masters have provided an interesting and useful imagery for the breath: both the in and the out breath should be long, thin and continuous, like a piece of never-ending thread. Another good piece of advice is not to use your nose like a suction pump; it is actually a smooth passageway for the flow of chi.

By following the above steps, all my chi kung students can perform Abdominal Breathing within two months. A useful guideline is to practise the breathing 36 times, followed by about 10 to 15 minutes of Standing Meditation. The whole training session takes about 20 to 30 minutes.

As with all the other chi kung exercises, the most important point is consistent, regular practice. It is useful to start your training with two or three dynamic chi kung patterns for five to ten minutes, follow this with Abdominal Breathing, and conclude with Standing Meditation. After six months of daily practice, you must be ready to hear your friends say that you have changed into a different (meaning healthier and livelier) person.

The Pathways of Energy Flow

When William Harvey published his *Movement of the Heart* in 1628 to describe blood circulation, Western medical scientists rightly hailed this as a momentous discovery. What these scientists were not aware of was that more than 2,500 years before this date, blood circulation was already known to the Chinese! The *Nei Jing*, or *Inner Classic of Medicine*, even differentiated the dark yin blood from the bright yang blood. What is even more amazing is their knowledge of a complex network of energy circulation, which the ancient Chinese knew in much greater detail than the circulation of blood. For the sake of humanity, let us hope that Western scientists will not take another 2,500 years to confirm such invaluable medical knowledge. The following description, though brief, will explain some important information about the energy circulation in the body.

Vital energy flows in our body in pathways called meridians, known as 'mai' in Chinese. Main meridians are called channels, or 'jing'; and sub-meridians are called collaterals, or 'luo'. But some books conventionally refer to channels as meridians and I shall do the same in this book.

There are two systems of channels or meridians, namely primary meridians and secondary meridians. Primary meridians pass through internal organs, but secondary meridians do not (because of this, ancient texts refer to them as 'wondrous').

There are 12 pairs of primary meridians flowing in continuous circulation through the following 12 organs in this order: lungs, colon, stomach, spleen, heart, intestines, urinary bladder, kidneys, pericardium, triple warmer, gall bladder and liver, then back to the lungs to resume the perpetual flow. Please refer to Figure 9.3 for the locations of the meridians.

Although the meridians are named according to organs through which they pass they do not refer to these organs only, but to complex, inter-related systems. So, if you complain of muscle pain in your back, do not be surprised if an acupuncturist tends to your urinary bladder meridian. This is because muscles are directly related to this meridian by an intricate system of energy circulation.

The triple warmer, a term which refers to the internal cavities at the chest, stomach and abdominal levels, is regarded as an organ in Chinese medicine. If we find this odd it is because of

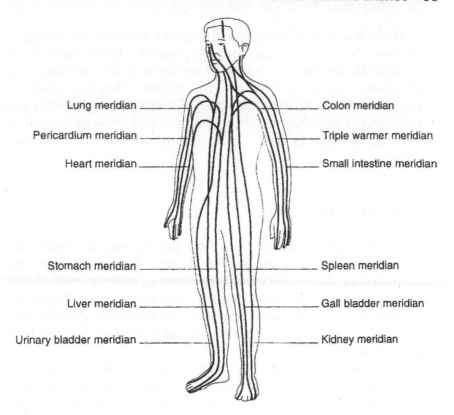

Lung meridian

Pericardium meridian

Heart meridian

Colon meridian

Triple warmer meridian

Small intestine meridian

Stomach meridian

Liver meridian

Urinary bladder meridian

Spleen meridian

Gall bladder meridian

Kidney meridian

Fig 9.3   The 12 Primary Meridians

our bias resulting from our familiarity with Western medical paradigms. Physiologically speaking, the triple warmer has more claim than many parts of our body, like the appendix or the rectum, to be called an organ. Its main functions include serving as a chi-filled buffer to protect other internal organs, facilitating the processes of peristalsis, food absorption and excretion, and promoting chi, blood and fluid circulation.

Closely connected with the triple warmer in the meridian system, is the 'pericardium', which in Chinese medical thinking, does much more than merely protect the heart. Ken, my Australian disciple, suggests that the Chinese term may actually refer to the thymus or the solar plexus, but, because of linguistic or other problems, it was first translated as 'pericardium' and the term has been in use ever since. Research into this area, combining Western technology with Chinese wisdom, may bring out some startling information.

There are points along the meridians where vital energy is focused, and where access is possible from outside to manipulate the internal energy flow. These points are known as acupoints, energy points or vital points. They are used by kungfu masters to injure their opponents using the dian xue (dim mark) or 'death-touch' technique; and by acupuncturists, massage therapists and chi kung masters in their healing systems.

A Reservoir of Energy

There are eight secondary meridians, namely ren, du, chong, dai, yin qiao, yang qiao, yin wei and yang wei. Translated into English they mean conceptual, governing, rushing, belt, in-tall, out-tall, in-protective and out-protective respectively. Except for the ren and du meridians (conceptual and governing meridians), which are located complementarily, all the other six meridians occur in pairs.

The ren and the du meridians, Figure 9.4, are the most important, with the ren meridian sometimes called 'the sea of yin energy', and the du meridian 'the sea of yang energy'. One of the greatest achievements in chi kung is to attain an

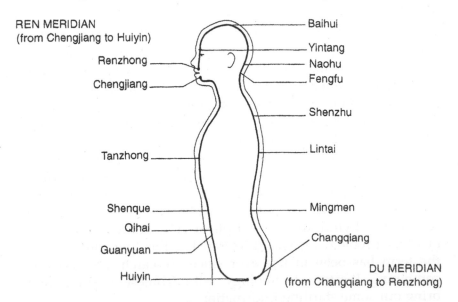

Figure 9.4   The Ren and Du Meridians

everlasting, continuous flow of energy along the ren and du meridians, known in chi kung terminology as the Small Universe or the microcosmic flow. From their long years of observation, chi kung masters in the past concluded that 'If you attain the breakthrough of the Small Universe, you will eliminate hundreds of illnesses. If you attain the breakthrough of the Big Universe, you will live to a hundred years.' The Big Universe or the macrocosmic flow refers to an everlasting, continuous energy flow throughout the 12 primary meridians.

The other six secondary meridians serve as elongated rays of energy protecting the body, as well as a reservoir to store reserved energy. When you are healthy, the extra energy you build up in your chi kung practice will be stored by the secondary meridians, to be used when needed. So, when the weather turns cold or when an epidemic occurs, you will still be warm or free from disease, as your reserved energy comes

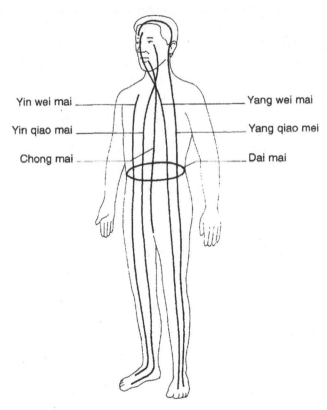

Yin wei mai

Yin qiao mai

Chong mai

Yang wei mai

Yang qiao mei

Dai mai

Figure 9.5   The Six Secondary Meridians

forward to serve you. Figure 9.5 shows the six secondary meridians.

As recently as 50 years ago, in the 1940s, many people would have laughed if you mentioned meridians or pathways of energy flow. Sceptics were quick to point out that surgeons could not find any meridians when they operated on their patients. They did not know that surgeons, and all of us, can only see a very small portion of reality. Our eyes are so limited that 'if the energy spectrum were a yardstick (36 inches; 91 centimeters), then what we see with our eyes in the small visible range would be less than a half inch (about 1.3 centimeters).'[1]

How, then, did chi kung masters know about meridians? Many of us may think that they gathered this knowledge through trial and error, discovering some vital points here and there, then through a long, gradual process spread over many centuries, linked these points into meridians. In reality, past masters discovered the whole system of meridians all at once, and the vital points were discovered later. These masters (independently) saw the meridians during deep meditation. Li Shi Zhen (1518–1593), one of greatest Chinese physicians whose Great Herbal Pharmacopoeia has become a classic, reported that in his meditation he saw an intricate network of energy flow. To attain such a psychic level certainly demands many years of chi kung practice; but if you practise Abdominal Breathing and meditation conscientiously, hopefully you may one day have some inner vision, or at least some sensation, of such energy flow. Meditation will be explained in more detail in the next chapter.

10

TRANQUILLITY OF JOY AND INNER PEACE

An Introduction to Meditation

❖ *Meditation for spiritual fulfilment is for those who are ready for this noble, sacred path. For most readers, however, the purpose and practice of meditation will be directed to daily needs.*

The Pathway to Our Greatest Achievement

What is the greatest achievement any person can attain? A happy life, being free from any worries, an everlasting piece of art, a breathtaking scientific invention, a medical breakthrough that will save countless lives, or a political masterpiece for world disarmament? Different peoples, depending on their upbringing and aspirations, will naturally give different answers. For me, in line with the highest Shaolin teaching and the supreme accomplishment in chi kung, a person's greatest achievement is his spiritual fulfilment, a direct personal experience of the Supreme Reality, an awareness of his origin and destiny, a realization of his immortality, where and when the whole universe and he *is*. The essential pathway to this enlightenment is meditation.

Although all the world's major religions appear to differ widely at the popular, ritualistic level, at the philosophical, spiritual level, as taught by their greatest teachers, all religions are similar.

Lao Tzu said, 'For us, who follow Tao, our ultimate aim is to be natural, spontaneous and merge with Tao'. What is Tao? Lao Tzu, the patriarch of Taoism, explained that Tao 'exists before heaven and earth, and has no form nor appearance. It is forever changing; and its constant transformation gives rise to form and appearance of everything in the universe.'[1] The way to merge with Tao is necessarily through meditation.

Hui Neng, the sixth patriarch of Zen Buddhism, said, 'If one wishes to follow religious practice to seek the Buddha outside, I do not know where he can find the real Buddha. If he can in his own mind see the real Buddha, that will bring about his realization of Buddhahood.' What is Buddhahood? Hui Neng explains, 'The pure nature of Supreme Reality is the real Buddhahood'.[2]

The Upanishads mention that 'the secret of immortality is to be found in purification of the heart, in meditation, in realization of the identity of the Self within and Brahman without. For immortality is union with God.'[3]

William James described Saint Teresa's union with God in her 'orison or meditation, the methodical elevation of the soul towards God', and emphasized that 'God establishes himself in the interior of this soul in such a way, that when she returns to herself, it is wholly impossible for her to doubt that she has been in God, and God in her'.[4]

The great Muslim master, Muhyyuddin Mohammed Ibn al-Arabi, said that 'there is no real difference between the Essence and its attributes, or, in other words, between God and the universe created by him'.[5] Another master, Mansur al-Hallaj, describing his experience of God during muraqaba or meditation, was even more direct; he exclaimed, 'I am He whom I love and He whom I love is I'.[6]

Meditation for spiritual fulfilment is for those who are ready for this noble, sacred path. For most readers, however, the purpose and practice of meditation will be directed to daily needs. The Venerable Dhammananada sums up the objectives of meditation succinctly:

> The immediate purpose of meditation is to train the mind and use it effectively and efficiently in our daily life. The ultimate aim of meditation is to seek release from the wheel of Samsara – the cycle of birth and death.[7]

It should be noted that whether we use meditation for prosaic demands or for divine aspiration, it is not two different types of meditation, but the same meditation. At the beginning of our inward journey, meditation enhances our natural abilities, making us perform better whatever we may do. At the advanced stage, the same meditation enables us to transcend space and time, transforming us from being human to being divine!

Different Levels of Meditation

Meditation is the cultivation of the mind to attain different levels of consciousness. In outward appearance, meditation is often performed seated on a chair or cross-legged on the ground with eyes closed or half closed, with the mind focused on one point or on nothingness. Nevertheless, meditation may be performed while standing, lying down or during bodily movement. The meaning of meditation is often interpreted differently at various levels of attainment.

For convenience of study we may divide meditation into four different levels, namely elementary, intermediate, advanced and divine. The difference between levels is one of degree rather than kind.

At the elementary level, meditation is primarily concerned with 'thinking nothing and doing nothing'. We sit cross-legged on the ground or upright on a comfortable chair. Alternatively, we may stand or lie down, or even perform some graceful movements like the chi kung exercises for induced chi flow described in Chapter 7.

The crucial point is to keep out distracting thoughts which drain off much of our mental energy. This is not an easy thing to do, but it can be done with practice, and with the help of techniques like the ones described later in this chapter. The mind becomes calm and alert, attaining a mental state known as 'the chi kung state of mind'. This is an efficient way to manage stress. At this stage we achieve physical, mental and emotional health.

As we continue to practise, we are able to keep our chi kung state of mind for longer and longer periods. We progress to the intermediate stage. The time needed to progress from the elementary level to this second level, or from any level to the next, depends on numerous factors, such as the natural ability of the meditator, the knowledge he has about meditation, the techniques and methods he uses, the guidance from his instructor, and the quality and quantity of his practice. It may range from a few days to a few years.

At this stage, the relaxed mind becomes very sharp and clear. Not only is mental energy conserved, but the mind also develops or generates further energy and focuses it one-pointedly. We produce better results in anything we set out to do. We may, if we know the techniques, use this level of deep consciousness to solve problems, or link our mind with the Universal Mind for inspiration and creativity. We may also have some control over our physiological and psychological functions.

As the mind journeys to the advanced level, it reaches altered states of consciousness and experiences different perceptions of reality. In this advanced chi kung state of mind, the mind transcends time and space, and may even shuttle between energy and matter. Hence it can perform feats that ordinary minds cannot, and which lay people, depending on their attitude, refer to as miracles or fakery.

Psychic powers and other special extraordinary abilities, such as clairvoyance, prediction, psychokinesis, distant healing and astral travel, are possible. The great chi kung master of China, Yan Xin, could change the molecular structure of various liquids 2,000 kilometres away! The great American psychic, Edgar Cayce, diagnosed and healed literally thousands of patients he had never met! It is understandable that most people would dismiss these cases as impossible, yet Yan Xin's experiments were carried out under the strict supervision of China's top scientists, and Cayce's documents (thousands of them) are still available for public investigation at the Association for Research and Enlightenment, Virginia.

The highest stage of meditation is the divine level, where a person accomplishes his greatest achievement, and where, as described above, the great teachers of the various religions attained their union with the Divine. Because of historical, linguistic and cultural differences, this spiritual fulfilment is described in different terms by people of different cultures. Christians call it the return to the Kingdom of God; Muslims, the return to Allah; Hindus, the union of atman with Brahman; Taoists, the unity with the cosmos; Buddhists, the attainment of nirvana or Buddhahood.

Why Do We Meditate?

We meditate for a great variety of purposes, which may be classified into five categories, namely health, clarity of thought, heightened creativity, supernormal abilities and spiritual development.

Meditation promotes health and longevity. It can cure and prevent a wide range of organic and psychosomatic diseases. It gives joyous tranquillity, and is excellent for managing stress.

Some readers may wonder how meditation, being motionless and passive, can cure illness. Meditation, it must be emphasized, is neither motionless nor passive. A meditative or chi kung state of mind can be attained while the body is in motion, as in Tai Chi Chuan and induced chi flow exercises. Even if the physical body is motionless, the mind may be actively involved in visualization. Even if the mind is stabilized into tranquillity, this state is reached after much direct and active mental effort. It is in such stillness of mind that our vital energy flows harmoniously, balancing yin-yang and cleansing meridians, hence curing illness and promoting health.

There is much evidence to show that meditation masters were not only healthy and fit, but lived to a ripe old age. For example, Zhang Bai Duan, whose *Realization of Truth* has become the Taoist classic describing how immortality is achieved through meditation, lived to the age of 98; while Sun Si Miao, the great Chinese physician who devised six wondrous chi kung sounds in meditation for healing, lived to 101.

By making our mind clear, fresh and one-pointed, meditation greatly increases our efficiency in our daily lives. We can produce better results in less time. We can also work for longer hours without feeling tired. Meditation is excellent for school and university students and those who frequently use their mental powers. Recently chi kung masters in China have classified a new genre of chi kung called intellectual chi kung, where meditation is a prominent aspect.

In addition to developing mental abilities, meditation enables us to link our mind with the Universal Mind, so that we can tap into the limitless wisdom of the cosmos. Inspiration, insight and creativity are enhanced. Indeed, all the great works of art, science and philosophy were produced in a meditative state of mind. Mozart, for example, would take rides into the countryside and hear wonderful music in his subconscious. Leonardo da Vinci would look meditatively into patterns of smoke from burning ashes, and inspiring ideas would flash upon his inner eyes.

Meditation develops psychic powers and other special extraordinary abilities, which were known in the past as miracles. For example, the great 16th century prophet, Nostradamus, in his meditative state of mind predicted events that have been proven true in our modern time. Since Dr Rhine's successful experiments at Duke University in the 1930s, which suggest that one in five people possesses psychic potential, many parapsychology departments, like those at the Universities of California and Cambridge, conduct courses to develop ESP.

Their methods, performed under scientifically controlled conditions, are surprisingly similar to those of classical chi kung masters, and their successes are heartwarming. In a pilot experiment on clairvoyance at Texas Southern University in 1977, for example, Lendell and William Braud recorded 36 direct hits with one hundred subjects, whereas the result by chance should be four times out of a thousand![8] In all training for acquiring ESP, whether following traditional techniques of classical masters or modern methods in research centres, a meditative state of mind is a necessary condition.

The supreme purpose of meditation is for spiritual development. Meditation, it is worth remembering, can be at different levels, and in different forms. It is not necessarily performed while seated cross-legged, with the body motionless and the eyes closed. When a devotee is in deep prayer, immersed in his recitation of scriptures, involved in religious rituals, or in personal communication with God, he is in meditation, for he has cultivated his mind to a different level of consciousness.

Standing Meditation

Meditation can be performed while standing, sitting, lying down or moving, but for those who are new to meditation, it is advisable to approach this fascinating art using the standing position.

Standing Meditation is comparatively safe, and the

practitioner can obtain results fairly quickly. Sitting Meditation, in a cross-legged or lotus position, leads to very deep levels of consciousness but it takes a longer time to achieve results. Sitting upright on a chair is a simplified form of the lotus position, which is particularly useful for those whose legs are too stiff to sit cross-legged, but its meditation effects are not as profound. Meditating while lying down is useful for those who are too old or sick to attempt other positions. Moving meditation is employed for special purposes, for example, to engender internal energy flow, or when it is easier for the practitioner to still his mind by first tagging it on some graceful movement.

Standing Meditation is a fundamental technique in Shaolin Chi Kung. A very good way to enter Standing Meditation is to use the first part of Abdominal Breathing, with the mind observing the rising and falling of the abdomen, as described on pp 76–79. The following technique is another excellent way to approach Standing Meditation.

Stand upright with your feet fairly close together. Drop your arms effortlessly to your sides, with elbows and fingers fairly straight and palms facing back. Close your eyes gently, and smile from your heart, Figure 10.1.

Keep your mind and body still. Empty your mind of all thoughts. As soon as any thought starts to enter your mind, throw it out gently but firmly. You will experience the void,

Fig 10.1 Standing Meditation

which is also full – a state of mind that is difficult to explain in words, and has to be experienced to appreciate its truth. Experience the resulting tranquillity of joy and inner peace.

After about ten minutes, or when you are satisfied with the practice, rub your palms together, and dab your warm palms on your eyes as you open your eyes. Massage your face gently, then walk briskly for about 30 steps to complete the exercise.

Sitting Meditation

When you are quite familiar with Standing Meditation, you may perform Sitting Meditation. It is advisable to start with the simplified sitting position.

Sit upright on a chair or stool with a fairly hard and flat surface, which must neither be too high nor too low so that your feet rest comfortably on the ground. Place your palms gently on your thighs or knees. Tilt your head slightly, and gently close your eyes. Relax and smile from your heart, Figure 10.2.

Empty your mind of all thoughts. When your mind is still, be gently aware of your breath. You need not make any effort to breathe in or out. Let your breathing be natural, but be gently mindful of your breaths. Your mind effortlessly follows your breath as it gently flows in and out.

Fig 10.2   Simplified Sitting Position

Fig 10.3   Single Lotus Sitting Position

After some time, often without you realizing it, your mind, breathing and body become one. Enjoy the tranquillity and inner peace for about five to ten minutes, or until you are satisfied with your practice.

Rub your palms together, and dab your palms on your eyes as you open your eyes. Massage your face gently and walk briskly for about 30 steps to complete the meditation exercise.

Later, if you feel comfortable enough, practise the meditation sitting cross-legged in the single (Figure 10.3) or double lotus position, that is, with the soles of one or both of your feet facing upwards respectively, with your palms resting on one another on your lap or both palms resting on your knees. Use a small, hard pillow or pad to sit on if necessary.

Useful Advice for Your Inward Journey

Whenever you practise meditation, you embark on a wonderful inward journey. Here is some advice to help you improve performance and avoid deviation.

- Practise regularly and consistently, once or twice a day, and whenever you need meditation to replenish your energy or calm your mind.
- Practise in a secluded area so that no one will disturb you. Loosen your belt and clothing during practice.
- Your body must be upright, but not tensed. You must be

physically and mentally relaxed. Your mind must be free from
irrelevant thoughts.

- Do not take a bath or a heavy meal within 15 minutes of your
  practice. Do not meditate near a cemetery, or when there is
  thunder and lightning.
- If there is a loud noise or any disturbance that violently jerks
  you from your meditation, reassure yourself that it cannot
  harm you, and think of your mind and vital energy being
  intact.

If you happen to see an unpleasant or frightening vision – an
occurrence that is unlikely to happen – gently but firmly order it
out of your mind. Should the vision continue to disturb you, rub
your hands, warm your eyes and complete the meditation.
Reassure yourself that it cannot harm you, and think of your
mind and vital energy being intact.

Meditation is an integral part of chi kung. Knowing the many
wonderful benefits that meditation can give, you may be
surprised at how apparently simple its methods are. Indeed, the
techniques needed to develop many fantastic abilities in chi
kung are actually quite simple, once you know them. The
difficulty lies in consistent, regular practice. The amazing thing
is not the simplicity of the techniques, but the wonderful
rewards you will inevitably get if you persevere.

11

DON'T WORRY EVEN IF THINGS GO WRONG

Deviations and Remedies

❖ *Any wrong practice, be it in sport, work or daily living, can bring unwanted side-effects. The harmful side-effects of chi kung are generally less serious than those of playing football, driving a car or taking medication for a prolonged period.*

Side-effects of Deviated Practice

Many chi kung students are afraid to practise any techniques other than those their instructors have taught them, or even to practise them in a different way, because they are worried that wrong practice may lead to serious harmful side-effects. This concern was accentuated in the past when information about chi kung was kept secret, and harmful side-effects were called by a descriptive but frightening term known as 'the escaping of fire and the entering of evil'.

It is true that wrong practice in chi kung can lead to harmful effects, but it is not as serious as many students imagine. The classical term about fire and evil is quite correct, although the effects it describes are not as serious as modern people might expect from the use of such a frightening term. 'Fire' here refers to the vitality of the body, and 'evil' to whatever is harmful, without necessarily having any moral or spiritual dimension. Thus the term means that, because of incorrect training, the vitality that should be developed, is missing, allowing things that are detrimental to health to occur. The modern, less frightening term is 'deviation'.

However, this does not imply that wrong or deviated chi kung practice will not be serious. Any wrong practice, be it in sport, work or daily living, can bring unwanted side-effects. The harmful side-effects of chi kung are generally less serious that those of playing football, driving a car or taking medication for a prolonged period.

If a student persistently practises chi kung incorrectly for a long time, despite tell-tale warnings, the result can be disastrous. The safeguards are the tell-tale warnings. If we heed them, we can easily remedy the deviations before they cause problems. In this chapter I will explain how to detect these warnings, and describe the remedial exercises to overcome the deviations. But we shall first examine two illuminating case histories which will give us a better understanding of deviations.

Injury from Forced Breathing

Chandran, a young man in his late twenties, practised 'Lifting the Sky' on his own without any guidance, not even from books. 'Lifting the Sky' is actually a very safe exercise, but this young man was extreme in his training. He breathed in forcefully, stretching the limits of his lungs, and tensed his muscles as he breathed out, as in some martial art chi kung training, under the wrong impression that this would build up his power rapidly.

After about three months of such wrong, forced training, he started vomiting blood. He became weak and languid. Specialists in two large hospitals could not find anything clinically wrong with him. 'All they told me,' he said, 'was I had over-strained myself, and I needed rest'. The doctors were right in saying Chandran had over-strained himself, but they could not find the cause of his illness because vital energy and energy blockage are not in their medical vocabulary.

Although Chandran's situation was grave, from the perspective of chi kung therapy the pathological and therapeutic principles involved are simple – if we know them. His consistent forced training had 'constricted' the meridians around his lungs and heart, resulting in blockage of energy flow to and from these organs. It was a blessing in disguise that he vomited blood, which was actually a tell-tale sign that something was seriously wrong. If he had not been 'strong' enough to vomit blood, or had the blood clotted internally, he might have died without knowing the reason.

Chandran's case was too acute to be treated by the holistic approach of chi kung therapy, where the same set of chi kung exercises can be used to relieve a wide range of different diseases. He needed the thematic approach, in which specific energy points and meridians directly related to the particular illness are treated. I opened a number of relevant energy points, and channelled my chi, or energy, into his affected meridians, first to clear the blockage, then to nourish his injured cells. He was cured after only a few sessions, within two weeks.

It must be emphasized that chi kung masters and chi kung therapists do not suggest that chi kung therapy is superior to conventional medicine. In many situations, such as acute contagious diseases, treatment by Western conventional medicine is better and speedier. In fact many chi kung masters and therapists advise their students or patients to consult conventional doctors before attempting chi kung therapy. But there are also situations, such as when a person has a degenerative disease, where chi kung therapy can offer a useful alternative treatment. We should also remember that curing illness is only one of the many benefits of chi kung.

Are They Real or Imaginary?

Mrs Cheah, a young mother in her thirties who practises chi kung with me, provides a different example. She was (and still is) a religious person, and had practised meditation for many years. However, she did not have much guidance in her religious meditation. She told me she often had headaches, and sometimes saw unpleasant and even frightening visions. Psychiatrists and religious teachers assured her that these visions were imaginary. She said she knew they were not real, yet they continued to distress her.

I told her that many of the fine meridians in her head were blocked. The blockages were probably due to her having disturbing thoughts while she meditated, and throughout her years of meditation these thoughts had generated forms of negative energy that had become trapped in the deeper recesses of her brain.

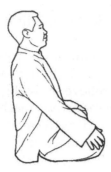

Fig 11.1   Faulty Position in Sitting Meditation

Another possible contributing factor was that as she progressed in her meditation, vital energy flowed up her spine from her lower energy field near the anus to her upper energy field at the top of her head. This flow of energy often makes the meditator sitting in the lotus position lean backward unconsciously, causing the head to tilt backward (Figure 11.1). In this way, the powerful energy flowing up the spine may enter the head at the naohu (gate of the brain) energy point, instead of flowing round the head to the 'baihui' (meeting of hundred meridians) energy point. This energy is therefore trapped inside the brain, and may press against certain cells or psychic centres producing visions.

It is ironical that this deviation does not occur in elementary students, but in advanced practitioners who have meditated long enough to generate energy flow up the spine, but who unfortunately do not have an understanding of the mechanics of the flow which would enable them to avoid the possible deviation. Mrs Cheah might have been a victim of such a deviated energy flow into her brain.

I surprised her and other people when I told her that her visions were not imaginary but real! They were not physical forms like ordinary objects, nor even astral forms like discarnate beings (for those who believe in non-physical beings); but they were not products of her imagination. They were trapped energy manifested as visions. That was why Mrs Cheah could not dispel them by an act of will.

While she performed Standing Meditation, I opened her relevant energy points, including those at her neck, chest, back, arms and legs. Then I channelled my chi into her head and, using my hand which maintained a chi-contact with her, flushed out her trapped energy. She went into some vigorous involuntary movements, and screamed occasionally. Some onlookers would probably be scared, thinking I was performing some exorcism, and some readers may dismiss this as nonsense. But there was nothing occult in this treatment; there were no evil spirits in her head. What I did was to cleanse her fine energy blockages and make her trapped energy flow.

Mrs Cheah continued to practise advanced courses in my chi kung class. Her headache and unpleasant visions have long since disappeared. Now she often has spiritual visions, in accordance with her religious beliefs. She has also developed some amazing psychic powers, which she does not pay much attention to. But the most amazing thing is that she also had cancer of the nose and this has been cured.

Causes and Symptoms of Deviations

Deviations occur when one or more of the three fundamental elements of chi kung – form, breathing and mind – are disharmonious. If we regulate or harmonize the form or posture, the breathing or flow of energy, and the mind in chi kung training, deviations will be effectively checked.

The causes of disharmonies may be qualitative or quantitative. A qualitative cause means that the quality of each chi kung pattern or movement is incorrect; a quantitative cause means the pattern or movement is repeated for too long a time causing harmful effects to set in. For example, breathing in too forcefully is a qualitative mistake; but gentle breathing carried on far too long becomes a quantitative error. This classification into qualitative and quantitative is for convenience only; in practice there is much overlapping.

The 'Do's and Don'ts' and 'Right Habits' explained in Chapter 6 also provide some useful advice to help prevent possible deviations.

The following list gives the common causes of deviations. The first two causes are due to disharmony of form, the next four to disharmony of breathing, and the last four to disharmony of mind.

1 Wrong, distorted or unbalanced posture.
2 Over-exertion in movements.
3 Forced breathing.
4 Forceful sinking of breath into the abdomen.
5 Insufficient breathing out.
6 Practising in a polluted environment.
7 Excessive anxiety over correctness of form.
8 Distracting thoughts during training.
9 Sudden, sharp noise that shatters peaceful concentration.
10 Harbouring evil thoughts.

Wrong, distorted or unbalanced posture affects the flow of chi or vital energy. The tell-tale sign is pain or discomfort. For example, if your back is slumped, chi may be blocked at the slumped area, causing pain. A person who is upright in posture and in character is unlikely to have deviations – in chi kung or in life.

All chi kung movements must be performed gently and gracefully unless the practitioner is instructed otherwise, as in some forms of martial art chi kung. Exertion of force may result in deviations. The over-exertion can be qualitative or quantitative. Physical tiredness and muscular tension are symptoms of forced movements. It is fascinating that no strength is applied in chi kung training, yet its effect can be very forceful.

As with the physical movements, all chi kung breathing must be gentle and graceful unless stated otherwise, as in some forms of martial art chi kung. Forced breathing, qualitatively or quantitatively, is a common cause of deviations among beginners, who erroneously think that more power is developed if they breathe forcefully or practise for a long time. A dry mouth or a feeling of thirst is often the symptom of forced breathing.

In certain chi kung techniques, such as Reversed Breathing where the chest instead of the abdomen is used, vital energy is lowered to the abdomen while breathing out. If this lowering of chi is performed too forcefully or vigorously deviation may happen. Pain in the groin is a sure sign of such deviation. If this deviated practice persists, a hernia or varicose veins may result.

Breathing out is as important as breathing in. At the elementary level, breathing out is even more important. If a student does not breathe out sufficiently (though it must be done gently and gracefully), 'stale' chi which is supposed to be expelled, may rise to his head, causing headaches and giddiness, two tell-tale warning signs of insufficient expiration.

If we realize that in chi kung training, we literally take in cosmic energy and give out stale energy from the body, we can better appreciate how important it is to practise in a clean, fresh environment. Practising in a polluted environment is tantamount to feeding our body cells with poison. Whatever good effects we derive from the practice will be offset by the poisonous intake. Our natural warning against this is feeling uncomfortable, suffocated, or dull.

Although correct form or posture is desirable, we must not be unduly worried about correctness of form, for this will result in unnecessary mental stress. The tell-tale signs are inattention, a distracted mind, giddiness or headache. Some allowance for individual differences or needs, and even minor mistakes, are permissible. As in form and breathing, disharmony of mind can be caused qualitatively or quantitatively. Prolonged effort to keep the mind relaxed becomes a stress.

Our mind should be free from irrelevant thoughts during training. Practising chi kung is actually an efficient way to eliminate distracting thoughts or mental problems. However, if you find your thoughts or problems persistently disturb your mind, it is better to stop training for the time being. Headache, giddiness, inattention and nervousness are symptoms of a distracted mind.

While you are in a meditative state of mind, a sudden loud noise or a sharp push by someone will not only shatter your peaceful concentration, but may also scatter your mind and energy. Subsequently you may feel nervous, anxious or easily frightened for no apparent reason. These are symptoms of scattered mind and energy. This can lead to very harmful consequences. Luckily, it is easy to prevent it, or to remedy it as soon as it happens. The injury occurs because you are taken by surprise. If you know the sound or disturbance will happen beforehand, the injury will be much minimized or even totally eliminated. You may not know when a sudden noise or disturbance may happen, but you can prepare for it, by telling yourself beforehand that when it happens, if it ever happens, it cannot harm you as it is only the bang of a door, the ringing of your telephone, the push of a friend, or whatever it is. If it does happen, immediately, by a firm act of will, keep your mind and energy intact. This can be done by firmly telling yourself that your mind is not scattered, nor your energy dispersed, and by feeling that your mind and energy are intact within you. Then take a few deep breaths, slowly and gently, and continue with your meditation.

Great masters have always advised that the highest attainment of chi kung can be reached only if our mind is clean and pure. An evil mind will produce evil energy that will first harm the practitioner. If a person's mind is full of hatred, malice or other negative thoughts, it will generate negative energy injurious to that mind, and may sometimes manifest on the face. This applies to all levels of chi kung, and is particularly significant at the advanced level where the energy involved is enormous and powerful. A sure sign of harbouring evil thoughts is losing the ability to laugh and love.

Remedies for Deviations

If the injury is new or not serious, it will often disappear once the deviation is corrected. For example, you feel pain in your chest, and after checking the list of possible causes of deviation you find that your chest was cramped when you practised chi kung, then by correcting your posture, thus promoting chi flow, you will soon eliminate the pain.

However, if you have an old or serious injury, correcting the deviation will prevent it from worsening but by itself may not be adequate to cure the injury. Remedial exercise will be necessary.

Listed below are the steps that you can follow to remedy your injury. They are arranged in order of procedure, though in some circumstances the order may be modified or some steps may not be necessary. Simple injury can be cured after the first few steps.

1 Consult your instructor.
2 Check possible causes.
3 Massage the injured part.
4 Channel chi to the injury.
5 Practise remedial dynamic patterns.
6 Practise induced chi flow.
7 Cure by breathing.
8 Cure by meditation.

If you suspect that you may have derived harmful effects from deviated training, discuss this with your instructor and ask him to check whether your training methods and procedures are correct. If a personal instructor is not available, discuss your problem with friends or other people who are knowledgeable about chi kung therapy.

Check the possible causes of deviation as well as the warning signs described above, one by one, and correct your mistakes. If, for example, you feel tired instead of fresh after each training, you may have over-exerted yourself either qualitatively or quantitatively. If you often feel thirsty, you may have forced your breathing.

Discomfort or pain is often due to incorrect posture, causing energy blockage. Rub your palms together to warm them, then massage the injured part to stimulate energy flow in that region. When the energy flow has cleared the blockage the discomfort or pain usually disappears.

If the energy blockage is deep, massaging the surface is inadequate and it is necessary to channel chi into the body. First focus your chi at your right or left palm. This can be achieved by rubbing the palms together, performing appropriate patterns such as Lifting the Sky or Big Windmill, or visualizing chi accumulating there while performing Standing Meditation. Next, place your palm over, but not touching, your injured area, and visualize chi flowing from your palm into it. Then move your palm around so that the transmitted chi from your palm massages the injury.

Performing the appropriate dynamic chi kung patterns will stimulate chi to flow to the injured area to cure it. For example, an injury to the back can be remedied by performing Carrying the Moon, and an injury to the waist by Merry-Go-Round. After repeating the required pattern sufficiently, go to Standing Meditation and feel chi flowing to the injured part to cure it.

Induced chi flow is a wonderful technique to remedy injury. In fact, if you practise induced chi flow regularly you will cure whatever injury you may have unwittingly sustained, or harmonize and enhance your energy level if you are not injured. During the induced chi flow, gently thinking of your injured part will direct your energy to flow there for healing.

Another effective method for more advanced students is to tap cosmic energy for healing. First perform Abdominal Breathing about 20 times. When cosmic energy is flowing smoothly from the universe into your body, direct the flow of cosmic energy to the injury for healing.

An advanced and effective technique is healing in meditation. Go into a deep level of consciousness, see the injury in your mind's eye, then work on it accordingly. Great power of concentration and visualization is needed for meditation healing.

An understanding of the causes of deviation and the remedies to overcome them is an essential part of an instructor's training. If an instructor is not knowledgeable and skilful in this area, it is difficult for him to teach students confidently and competently, for he has to face the possibility and bear the responsibility that one day some of his students may develop harmful side-effects due to deviated practice. For students, a knowledge of deviations and skill in dealing with them qualify them to move one class higher than the uninformed, for not only are they able to heal themselves should deviations happen, but with the better perspective it gives them they can now dare to modify what they have learnt to suit their individual needs. Thus they can take the first step away from mere studentship towards becoming future masters should they have the perseverance to travel on.

MEET THE MASTERS AND KNOW THEIR ARTS

Some Popular Types of Chi Kung Outside China

❖ *Before we practise the art, we must practise virtue. Virtue is the foundation. If we emphasize virtue, we will be successful in our art.*

The Contemporary Scene

Did you know that the founder of a very popular chi kung today is a Muslim? Or that a recent discovery by a chi kung master regarding 'disease data' in the brain may hold the key to some pressing medical problems?

Just 30 years ago, if you mentioned chi kung most people would not understand what you were talking about, even though chi kung has been practised since ancient times. This was because in the past chi kung was kept secret; the very few people who knew about it often associated it with advanced kungfu.

One of the earliest types of chi kung popularly practised outside China, especially in South-East Asia where overseas Chinese are predominant, was Waitankung. In the 1980s Waitankung instructors taught large public groups, charging only nominal fees. Because Waitankung served a useful social function, and its instructors were non-profit-making, many respectable Chinese associations, like the Moral Uplifting Societies in Malaysia and Singapore, organized Waitankung classes.

Later, another type of chi kung, called Taiji Eighteen Steps became very popular. Like the Waitankung instructors before them, Taiji Eighteen Steps instructors also taught their art for a nominal fee. Its rapid increase in popularity was due to its health benefits as well as to its easy accessibility. Anybody, irrespective of race and religion, could simply walk in and join any one of the many groups practising Taiji Eighteen Steps in public open spaces.

As both Waitankung and Taiji Eighteen Steps emphasize the health aspect of chi kung, virtually without touching on the martial aspect, many people nowadays mistakenly believe that chi kung is only for health – a reverse of the situation 30 years ago. Still fewer people imagine that chi kung could also be useful for mental and spiritual development.

Other popular chi kung types include Damo Chi Kung, Chanmizong Chi Kung, Flying Crane Chi Kung, Shaolin One-Finger Zen Chi Kung, Taoist Chi Kung, Taiji Chi Kung, and Shaolin Cosmos Chi Kung.

Waitankung

Waitankung, meaning 'the Art of External Elixir', provides a very good example of the non-religious nature of chi kung. It was founded by a Muslim, based on Taoist philosophy, spread by Confucianists, and is now practised by people of different races and religions. The Grandmaster, Sifu Zhang Zhi Tong, who rediscovered Waitankung is a Chinese Muslim living in Taiwan.

Waitankung originated from the advanced chi kung of Tongbi Kungfu (meaning 'Kungfu of Through-Arm'). In 1949, about ten years before the modern term 'chi kung' was coined, Sifu Zhang rediscovered Waitankung from a secret kungfu text which he had inherited from his master years earlier. The following summary illustrates some of the interesting aspects he experienced when he first practised the 12 patterns of the art.[1]

After practising the first pattern, 'he felt as if his heart would jump out of his body, his whole body aching, his legs weak, his head and eyes giddy, and he felt like vomiting.' But these symptoms disappeared half an hour later, and he felt energetic.

After the second pattern, he was surprised at his strength when he performed his Tongbi Kungfu. He found it almost unbearable to hold his stretched arms in the fourth pattern for 30 seconds; yet he persevered for over an hour. 'Suddenly he felt as if his hands were charged with electricity.' The fifth pattern made his hearing very sharp.

When he practised the sixth pattern, he experienced electric impulses flowing along his spine. He explained that the next three patterns promote chi flow, the tenth pattern promotes joint movements, and the eleventh pattern prevents elderly people from suffering 'wind illness' (paralysis). The twelfth pattern enables the student to walk for long distances without feeling tired.

The diagrams showing the twelve patterns of Waitankung, Figure 12.1, are meant to suggest their form; they are not meant for self-instruction. Readers who wish to pursue this art should contact qualified Waitankung instructors.

Three Fields and Nine Palaces

The Grandmaster himself explains the principles and practice of Waitankung in the following way.

> For the practice of Waitankung, first arouse your pre-natal energy,[2] loosen and stretch your limbs and body, then practise the various patterns to enable circulation of blood and energy without hindrance. Gradually increase the energy of your body, with the result that your internal organs become genial and you become naturally healthy and comfortable.
>
> The pre-natal energy of Waitankung flows in your body like electric impulses, making you 'sway'. This 'swaying' is because of chi. The body and the four limbs are filled with chi, making you cheerful in your heart, pleasant in your body, and peaceful in your mind. As the whole body becomes comfortable, and the internal organs genial, you are naturally healthy and will enjoy longevity.
>
> It is necessary that you must have patience and perseverance in the practice of the twelve patterns of Waitankung. In the process, there may be discomfort. This is an occurrence of reaction-symptom, and if you endure, the symptom will disappear and you will later feel comfortable.
>
> After two years of training, the pre-natal energy of Waitankung naturally changes into 'elixir energy',[3] which can promote longevity. If you 'train chi (energy) to become shen (spirit)', you may enter sainthood. In Waitankung training, 'fluid generates essence, essence generates energy, and energy generates spirit'.[4] Essence, energy and spirit react with one another in your three energy fields. [These three energy fields are found at the top, middle and bottom levels of a

Fig 12.1   The 12 Patterns of Waitankung

person.][5] If you practise long enough, you may acquire supranormal abilities.

The pre-natal energy of Waitankung does not only react in the three energy fields, but, if practised long enough, also flows through the nine palaces. Where are the nine palaces? They are located at the kidneys, intestines, liver, gall bladder, spleen, colon, lungs, urinary bladder and heart.[6] When the pre-natal energy flows into the nine palaces, after more than a year it can nourish the brain and enrich the marrow; after three years it can make an old person rejuvenated to become a child.[7]

It is interesting to note that while most Waitankung students may not be aware of it because they have not progressed to the advanced level, the Grandmaster clearly indicates that Waitankung is applicable for martial art training as well as for mental and spiritual development.

Taiji Eighteen Steps

Taiji Eighteen Steps Chi Kung is different from Tai Chi Chuan (Taijiquan) and traditional Taiji Chi Kung. It is so named because this art is based on the graceful and gentle features of Tai Chi Chuan, and the three harmonies of essence, of energy and of mind in chi kung philosophy. It was invented in 1981 by a famous chi kung master and Chinese physician from mainland China, Sifu Lin Hou Sheng. Sifu Lin also made other startling contributions to the modern development of chi kung. In 1978, he transmitted chi to scientific instruments which registered infra-red radiation, proving for the first time in history that chi has material reality.[8] In 1980, he successfully used chi, and nothing else, as anaesthesia on 11 patients while they underwent major surgical operations![9]

Regarding the principles and practice of Taiji Eighteen Steps, let the Grandmaster himself explain.

Why is it that those who regularly participate in sports and chi kung training have rosy cheeks, well-formed bodies, are not scared of cold in winter nor heat in summer, and are seldom sick; whereas those who are untrained are pale, scared of cold and heat, and easily become ill? This is because the essence of the former is strong, that of the latter is weak. From the perspective of Chinese medical philosophy, the former are full of vital energy, which the latter lack.

Vital energy is the basis of health. 'If evil attacks a person, it is certain that his vital energy is insufficient.' 'If vital energy is present, evil cannot enter.' ('Vital energy' refers to a person's natural resistance to illness; 'evil energy' refers to all disease-causing agents.) This shows that illness occurs not only because of disease-causing agents, but also because of a person's natural resistance.

Taiji Eighteen Steps is able to prevent illness because it strengthens a person's essence, enhances vital energy and promotes his natural resistance ... A person's health is closely related to emotional stress ... Taiji Eighteen Steps makes use of congenial feelings combined with pleasant thoughts of beautiful scenery, and a relaxed and cheerful attitude to overcome various irrelevant thoughts, anxiety and agitated feelings ...

Through practising Taiji Eighteen Steps, we can cleanse our meridians and harmonize the circulation of blood and energy, thus achieving the functions of preventing and curing dieases ... After practising Taiji Eighteen Steps for some time, we can gradually improve the co-ordinating functions of our sympathetic and parasympathetic nervous systems ... Changes in the internal environment of our abdomen 'massage' our stomach, colon and intestines, promoting their movements and improving their digestive and absorptive functions ...

People have a lot of potentialities that are not properly developed. Many capillaries in a person's body are often in a state of blockage. A person has about 140 billion nerve cells in his brain; only between 10 and 20 billion cells are frequently used, hence between 80 and 90 per cent of the nerve cells have never been properly developed. A person has about 7.5 billion lung cells, but only a portion is frequently employed. After practising Taiji Eighteen Steps, there is noticeable increase in brain wave activity, lung intake capacity, and blood flow volume. This shows that Taiji Eighteen Steps can develop a person's potentialities.

When a person's essence, energy and spirit are good, he is healthy.[10] Through harmonizing the body, the breathing and the mind while practising Taiji Eighteen Steps, we harmonize all the internal functions of our body, emphasize mind training, stress the unity of spirit and body, improve and strengthen our essence, energy and spirit, thus increasing vitality and self resistance, curing illness and promoting health.[11]

Figure 12.2 shows the 18 patterns of Taiji Eighteen Steps Chi Kung. Readers who wish to practise this chi kung should learn from a qualified instructor.

The Grandmaster's Advice

Sifu Lin Hou Sheng provides the following advice for Taiji Eighteen Steps training.[12]

1 Persevere in your training. Do not drop out half way. Have faith, determination and patience.
2 Maintain correct posture throughout the training. The body should be relaxed, upright and natural. Movements should be gentle, circular, fluid and co-ordinated.
3 Pay attention to the functions of mind and breathing. There are three aspects of the art: training of posture, of mind, and of breathing. Think of a pleasant scene for each pattern, such as admiring the moon. Breathing should be deep.
4 Pay attention to 'internal force'. 'Use mind; do not use mechanical strength. Use will to lead the flow of chi.' When external form moves (without strength), internal force flows.
5 Movements should be light and pleasant, fluid and continuous. Practise with a smile, and with background music. There should not be any abrupt break between changes of pattern.
6 Practise in a comfortable, quiet and scenic environment. Outdoor practice is not suitable if it is too windy. If you practise indoors, ensure that the air is fresh. Practise one to three times a day, for about 15 minutes each time.

Fantastic Attainments of Shaolin Damo Chi Kung

Some years ago, a highly respected chi kung master who was almost a hundred years old was invited to speak to an audience of several thousand people at a national chi kung conference in China. 'I'm not a good speaker,' he said modestly, 'perhaps I could demonstrate, instead'. Despite his age, he was as fit as a kungfu expert of 50. He looked around and saw a paralysed man in a wheel-chair. 'Please bring that gentleman on stage,' he said.

The paralysed man was laid on a table and the master stood a

Fig 12.2   Taiji Eighteen Steps

few feet from him. The master moved his hands about in the air, in the direction of the patient. After a short while the patient started to move his limbs, slowly at first, but gradually the movements became faster and more vigorous. The patient's movements seemed to be controlled by the master, as if there were invisible strings for the master to manipulate him like a huge puppet. Everyone in the hall watched in stunned silence. This, however, was not the most amazing part of the impromptu demonstration.

After about 15 minutes of directed, spectacular movements by the patient, who was sweating profusely while the master remained calm and relaxed, the master asked some helpers to make the paralysed man stand up. After some initial hesitation, encouragement and prodding, and accompanied by thunderous applause, the patient walked away from the stage unaided! If you find this report unbelievable, as many reports of chi kung feats are, be prepared for more surprises.

This old master is Sifu Ou Bao Xiang, the current Grandmaster of Shaolin Damo Chi Kung. Damo is the Chinese name for Bodhidharma, the great Indian monk who arrived at the Shaolin Monastery in China in 527 and initiated Chan (Zen) Buddhism, Shaolin Kungfu and Chi Kung.

Sifu Ou Bao Xiang's overseas inner-chamber disciple[13] is Sifu Chin Chee Ching, who lives in Singapore and has spread the art to Malaysia, Taiwan, Hong Kong, Vietnam and Thailand.

Sifu Chin's free chi kung seminars are as exciting as a magic show. As a demonstration, Sifu Chin stands more than ten feet behind some volunteers who have no chi kung experience. When he gently moves his palm forward, the volunteers, who do not know what the master is doing, move forward too, pushed by the master's chi. When the master pulls back his palm, the volunteers retreat a few steps, pulled by the master's invisible force. Sometimes this feat is demonstrated by his students, who have practised chi kung with him for only a few months!

The main purpose of the seminars, of course, is not a magic show, but to cure illness and accept new students. If you have an illness, he will cure it free of charge. If you wish to be his student (and if he accepts you), you will have to pay a fee, which, depending on your attitude, may be interpreted as very high or very economical. If you compare it with the nominal fees charged by many public chi kung classes, if is high; but if you think in term of cost-effectiveness, it is very economical. Students can gain as much benefit from him in one hour as they would in many years at chi kung classes elsewhere!

How is this possible? Sifu Chin accomplishes this feat by doing his students a great service; by opening for them three important energy points, which are usually three of the following: baihui (meeting of hundred meridians), naohu (house of brain), fengfu (residence of wind), or lingtai (spiritual platform) and mingmen (gate of life). When these points are open – an attainment which may take years of personal practice without a master's help – vital energy flows harmoniously along the student's spine.

For the Benefit of All Humanity

Sifu Chin explains:

> The typical feature of Damo Chi Kung is that the master can use special techniques to open the students' three energy points, to harmonize their internal energy and to transmit his own energy into them. The students, in a chi kung state of mind, attend chi kung classes, train diligently, tap cosmic energy for internal flow, and channel vital energy throughout the body to harmonize yin-yang and cleanse meridians. In this way, energy is developed powerfully and fast. Within a week, students can transmit energy to help others and themselves to cure illness. The advantages of Damo Chi Kung are simplicity of its methods for easy learning, balance of internal and external training, no need for mental focus, no deviations, not being limited by time, age, or sex, and convenience for practice at any time of the day.
>
> Besides the typical features and advantages mentioned above, other extraordinary lessons include how to transmit chi impulses into water, how to place impulses inside and outside houses, on patients, on clothing or on any objects;[14] and how to diagnose and cure illness 10,000 miles away. More amazing still is the transmission of 'chi kung needles' 10,000 miles away (which is a figurative way to say, opening a patient's vital points from a great distance), opening of a child's 'heavenly eye' so as to enhance his intelligence, breaking down of stones in the kidney or gall bladder, lowering hypertension and reducing high fever, as well as teaching

'marvellous electricity chi kung'[15] which is excellent for curing rheumatism, 'art of strengthening kidneys',[16] 'art of heavenly eye and longevity' and 'art of fragrance'.[17]

As I have mentioned earlier, many of the developed abilities of chi kung masters are simply incredible. I would like to repeat an important point in Shaolin philosophy, shared by both Sifu Chin's Shaolin Damo Chi Kung and my Shaolin Cosmos Chi Kung: do not accept anything on faith alone, nor on the reputation of the master, but practise diligently with an open mind, then evaluate the teachings according to your experience.

Sifu Chin Chee Ching is a sincere, soft-spoken master of 60. His aim is to enable all people of the world to enjoy the benefits of chi kung. His genuine care for people is clearly shown in his motto: 'Saving another person's life is saving my own life', which also reflects two principal features of Shaolin philosophy, namely compassion and universality.

'Another person's life is my own life' – in the spirit of Chan (Zen), which originated from Damo (Bodhidharma) – is not just regarding another person as your brother; it is transcendental. It means that when in our meditation we see Reality as undifferentiated, non-dualistic, there is really no difference between any other person or thing and us, no difference between object and subject whatsoever. It is in such a deep level of consciousness that the many incredible feats in Shaolin Damo Chi Kung, and in any chi kung, become attainable.

If you find Shaolin Damo Chi Kung fascinating, you can contact Sifu Chin Chee Ching, not to seek proof of the fantastic attainments mentioned above (most chi kung masters are not concerned whether other people believe their achievements or not), but to learn from him and, hopefully, help him to spread the goodness of chi kung to all humanity. His address is given at the end of the book.

What are the requirements for someone wishing to become a student of chi kung? The most important condition required by Sifu Chin is virtue.

Before we practise the art, we must practise virtue. Virtue is the foundation. If we emphasize virtue, we will be successful in our art. We must have clear philosophical teaching. The saying goes: false instructions can be transmitted by millions of books, truth can be transmitted by just one word. In learning, practising, and applying chi kung, we must bear in mind the popular sayings of chi kung philosophy, namely 'When the heart is righteous, the art is successful', 'The beneficial results of the art are limitless', and 'Be courteous, righteous, perfect and open'.[18]

'Forced' to be a Chi Kung Therapist

At 36, Sifu Yap Soon Yeong is one of the youngest chi kung masters in the world; he is also one of the most successful. His recent discovery of 'diseased chi' in bone marrow, and 'memories of disease' in the brain – a discovery that even elderly masters had not made before – may turn out to be a break-through in chi kung thinking and practice.

Despite his youthfulness, Sifu Yap has taught and practised martial arts, chi kung and meditation for more than 20 years. He holds a third dan black belt in International Shorinryu Yongshikan Karate, and was a former instructor of Praying Mantis Kungfu.

Sifu Yap was 'forced' to become a professional chi kung healer. He was a fully qualified public accountant and approved company auditor. In 1980, after being taught mind-power development and psychic healing by a harta yoga master, he started curing people in his spare time. During this period he also practised several types of chi kung, and read extensively on human anatomy, meridians and Buddhism. For nine years he gave free healing, and was so successful that his house was crowded every day.

I can still remember what Sifu Yap told me in 1989. 'I have no choice,' he said. 'There are so many patients – they come every day, every minute – that I can't do any other work. And I can't turn them away; they need my help. So I have to give up my accountancy and practise chi kung therapy full-time.'

If you wonder how a chi kung therapist treats patients, you should visit Sifu Yap's therapy centre where you can see numerous techniques at work. First, you will be impressed by the professional way Sifu Yap keeps records of patients' particulars, symptoms, therapeutic methods applied and results observed. You may find the master transmitting chi to many patients at the same time, with the patients swaying or moving in different, sometimes spectacular, actions, and apparently enjoying themselves. Sometimes a patient may lie on a bed while the master dots his finger over him, opening the patient's energy points.

Sifu Yap uses the principles of meridians and five elemental processes. If the patient's disease is caused by blockage of the heart and the intestine meridians, for example, the master will clear the meridians in various ways. Sometimes it may be better to treat the disease using an indirect method, instead of treating the respective meridians directly. For example, a particular illness may be caused by sluggish chi flow in the lung meridian. Instead of trying to increase chi flow in the lung meridian (which does not have much chi in the first place), an alternative and often better approach is to stimulate the healthier spleen system, which can indirectly improve the lung system. This is applying an aspect of the five elemental processes: of earth (representing spleen) nourishing metal (lung).

How does Sifu Yap clear blockages, stimulate chi flow, and produce other therapeutic effects? He uses a range of techniques including non-contact chi transmission, acupressure, vital point stimulation and massage therapy, which he may use singly or in combination.

Sifu Yap is renowned for healing knee problems, ankle problems, back pains, sciatica, migraine and neck and shoulder stiffness. Recently he has been successful in curing ankylosing spondylitis (hardening of the backbone) and tinnitus (ringing sounds in the ear).

In treatment, Sifu Yap emphasizes thorough cure. He said, 'Most patients with chronic ailments may have multiple problems, though they may only complain of one particular disturbing problem. For example, a patient complaining of pain in a knee may also have pain in the other knee, backache, constipation, flatulence, neck and body stiffness, frequent headache and tiredness. Healing is not complete if only the pain in the knee is removed, as often all these problems are inter-connected. If all the other problems are not cured, it is likely that the knee problem will recur soon. In fact, when treatment is complete, the patient experiences an overall well-being – eat better, sleep well, walk faster, feel lighter.'

Sifu Yap advises patients who receive chi kung treatment to stop all medication, drugs or food supplements unless these are necessary to control the ailments, for example, in the case of high blood pressure or diabetes. He notices that patients who have been taking fewer supplements normally have less complicated problems, and those who stop taking supplements normally heal faster.

You don't have to be sick to benefit from Sifu Yap's skills. In addition to giving therapy, he also teaches Micro-Cosmic Meditation, Shaolin Neichin It-Tze Zen (Internal Force of Shaolin One-Finger Zen), and Zhonghua Ziran Tonglin Chi Kung (Chinese Natural Psychic Chi Kung). So readers seeking for more power in sports and games, more vitality in work and play, or more life in their years and more years in their life, will get much help from one of Sifu Yap's many arts.

Sifu Yap's Exciting Discovery

A breakthrough happened in December 1992, which may have a significant place in chi kung history. While practising the Tibetan Mahamudra Yoga, Sifu Yap saw in his deep meditation the conditions of chi in his patients' bone marrow and brains! This indeed is an exciting revelation, one of the most beautiful instances of intuitive wisdom, where masters come face to face with reality in a mystical, almost divine experience which often results in a subsequent discovery which brings much benefit to humanity. I rejoiced with Sifu Yap as he briefly described his discovery to me over the phone, and he was also kind enough to explain it to me later in a long letter.

While Sifu Yap had previously worked on the meridians and internal organs of his patients, because of his discovery he is now able to penetrate into their bone marrow and brain. As far as I know, this is the first time any chi kung master anywhere in the world has viewed chi and illness in this manner. What is most exciting about 'Yap's theory of diseased chi in the brain' is the possibility that it could be further developed by him, or by other great minds, and that it may lead to the solution of many pressing medical problems. The excitement of his startling discovery is best shared in his own words.

> The more concentrated diseased chi exists in the bone marrow. While cleaning up the chi in the meridians and blood vessels may cure the ailments for several years, a more lasting cure may be

possible if the diseased chi in the bone marrow is cleaned up.

Certain 'memories', 'information' or 'data' of diseases must be removed from the brain tissues to result a perfectly thorough cure.

Chi that works in (a) meridians, vessels, internal organs, (b) bone marrow, and (c) brain are of different qualities. In (a) a patient can easily feel the chi transmitted, in some cases develops spontaneous movements,[19] and the healer can control the physical movements of the patient.[20]

In (b), spontaneous movements rarely happen but the patient may feel intense heat and ache.

In (c), no spontaneous movements, not much chi sensation, but the patient feels relaxed. About half such patients will doze off or yawn continuously during the treatment. When they are allowed to lie down they quickly fall asleep. Almost all patients acquire the 'yearning for sleep syndrome' subsequent to the treatment, which may last for one week. The removal of 'unhealthy signals' from the brain results in a thorough adjustment to the body system. Blocked channels are cleared up and 'lazy tissues' are re-activated. Within 1–5 sessions, patients normally experience pains/aches all over the body, especially places which had previous trouble. Some patients experience a series of such adjustment throughout the duration of treatment.[21]

'Yap's theory of diseased chi in the brain' prompts me to ask the following questions:

1 Does this theory satisfactorily provide useful information to support the ideas which many Western doctors are now beginning to believe, and which most Eastern healers have long believed, that illness starts in the mind?
2 As well as cancer and Aids, there are many other fatal diseases that are considered 'incurable' based on present medical knowledge. Can Yap's theory lead us to view these diseases from different angles, perhaps resulting in some cure?
3 Can we, irrespective of the type of medical philosophy we hold, afford not to consider these questions?

Hopefully, some brave minds will take up the challenge of these questions. Sifu Yap, I am sure, will be ready to help. His address is given at the end of this book.

13

INCURABLE DISEASES CAN BE CURED!

Chi Kung and Chinese Medicine

❖ *There are diseases, especially degenerative diseases that conventional medicine regards as incurable, that can be cured by practising chi kung. This claim is based not on the experiences of a few isolated patients but on hundreds of cases.*

Hundreds Have Been Cured

The claim in the title of this chapter is made earnestly and sincerely. It is not a challenge to those who disagree, for everyone has a right to their opinion. It is definitely not a slight on conventional Western medicine, whose doctors, basing their understanding on their training and their present philosophy, generally maintain that many of the diseases chi kung claims to cure are incurable. I always have great respect and much gratitude for conventional Western medicine. It has, for instance, enabled me, my wife and all my five children to come into this world safely, and has looked after the health of my children extremely well.

Nevertheless, there are diseases, especially degenerative diseases that conventional medicine regards as incurable, that can be cured by practising chi kung. This claim is based not on the experiences of a few isolated patients but on hundreds of cases. There are literally hundreds of people, including many conventional doctors, who have been relieved of their so-called incurable diseases, such as hypertension, heart problems, asthma, peptic and duodenal ulcers, arthritis, rheumatism, diabetes, kidney failure, insomnia, and even cancer, after practising chi kung.

This is a fact, though I have not kept detailed records of all these recoveries. Most people do not even keep records of their own illnesses, let alone those of other people. There are numerous people whom I have saved from dying, yet did not even ask their names. What I am particularly concerned about is that for each person cured, there are hundreds of others suffering the same illness who are not aware of the availability of a healing system that has been proved effective.

I do not suggest that every patient will certainly be cured if he practises chi kung. No responsible person can guarantee recovery, because this depends on other factors in addition to the therapeutic method – factors that are often beyond the control of the therapist. But I can say that of the hundreds of patients who suffered from these so-called incurable diseases who have practised chi kung consistently from me or my disciples, more than 80 per cent of them have their illness relieved and do not suffer any relapse. Masters of other types of chi kung also have remarkable results.

There are sound principles in Chinese medical philosophy to explain how and why chi kung and other branches of Chinese medicine cure illness. Chi, or energy, is the basic consideration in the diagnosis, pathology, therapeutics and other aspects of all branches of Chinese medicine, including herbalism, acupuncture, massage therapy and physiotherapy. It is in chi kung therapy that chi is employed most directly.

But because the philosophy of Chinese medicine is totally different from that of Western medicine, and Chinese medical principles are explained in terms unfamiliar to most people, including many Chinese, the public in general do not understand them.

Even some chi kung masters themselves, who may be very skilful in their practice, are ignorant of chi kung therapeutic principles. It is not surprising, therefore, that an air of mystery hangs over chi kung therapy, which unfortunately hampers a wider and deeper public involvement in this fascinating art.

Some Glimpses of Chinese Medical Philosophy

It is worth reminding ourselves that Western medical philosophy is only one of the many ways of looking at health and illness. Long before Western medical knowledge and practice became a science, other medical philosophies, such as those of the Egyptians, Greeks, Arabs and Indians, as well as that of the Chinese, had served their peoples effectively for ages. Each of these had its own concepts and, just as it is inappropriate to use English grammar in Sanskrit or Arabic, it is inapplicable to explain Chinese medical principles using Western medical concepts. Hence it is as irrelevant to ask a Chinese physician how he would cure a patient complaining of a headache caused by a malignant brain tumour, as it is to ask a Western doctor how he would treat a patient with symptoms of insufficient yin due to excessive fire at the inner level of his head. This does not mean the doctors or physicians are helpless when faced with such diseases or symptoms; they will interpret the diseases or symptoms according to the paradigms they are trained in, and will attend to their patients according to their abilities.

It is the misunderstanding of terms such as yin and yang, fire and inner level, that cause many people to conclude, erroneously, that Chinese medicine is non-scientific. These terms do not refer to any specific bodily parts nor pathogenic agents; they are symbols that are effectively used to describe complex situations in a very concise way. Let us examine them briefly.

Yin and yang refer to the two opposing yet complementary aspects of reality. For example, Chinese physicians sum up all the mechanisms of our body defence systems as yin, and all the external disease-causing agents as yang. Although we are immersed in a sea of pathogenic micro-organisms, we are not sick because our natural defence systems can counter these disease-causing agents. This is described as the harmony of yin-yang. However, if our defence systems are weakened, for example, by worry or fatigue, then we may become sick, although the amount or potency of the pathogenic micro-organisms has not changed. This disharmony is described as insufficient yin.

On the other hand, our yin defence may remain the same, but if the pathogenic micro-organisms increase in amount or potency, such as in an open wound, or when contaminated food has been consumed, then we may become sick. This is excessive yang.

In Chinese physiology, substance is referred to as yin, and function as yang. If you suffer from gastric pain because your stomach produces too much gastric juice, then the cause of your illness is described as excessive yang. On the other hand, your stomach may function normally, but if you take too much food or food that is too rich, you may become ill, and this is described as excessive yin. In all cases, health can be restored when we restore the harmony of yin-yang.

Fire is a common symbolic term in Chinese medicine. In pathology, it can refer to one of the 'six evils'. These six evils have no religious connotations, but figuratively refer to the six major classes of external agents that cause diseases. In physiology, it can refer to the body's metabolic processes.

Fire is also one of the five elemental processes, which are frequently and wrongly interpreted as the five elements. These five processes are metal, water, wood, fire, and earth. They are not the basic elements that make up the universe; rather they refer to five archetypes of processes. Of course, there are countless different processes in real life, but Chinese scientists and philosophers discovered that all these myriad and varied processes can be classified into five archetypes, and that there is a distinct relationship between these processes.

Chinese physicians discovered that, based on their typical behaviour and reaction, the various internal organs can be described by these elemental processes. For example, the liver is figuratively described as wood, and the heart as fire – not that the liver is made of the element wood, nor the heart the element fire; but because the typical behaviour and reaction of the liver and the heart resemble the wood and the fire processes.

From long years of study, Chinese physicians discovered that when a person is angry it affects his liver, and if he continuously loses his temper he weakens his heart. Chinese physicians described this tendency figuratively, as excessive wood creates excessive fire. In simple language, it means that if you are easily prone to anger, you are more likely to suffer a heart attack. It is not because some philosophers had previously said that wood creates fire, that Chinese physicians conclude that excessive anger may lead to heart attack. It is the other way round.

Chinese physicians had discovered the connection first, then they used the wood and fire symbols to express this observation concisely.

A very interesting and rewarding application of this concept of the five elemental processes is in the treatment of psychiatric or emotional disorders. (Emotional disorders will be discussed in the next chapter.) Chinese medical records are full of fascinating case histories which show the effective use of the interplay of these five elemental processes, and nothing else, to cure diseases where modern doctors would resort to anti-depressants, tranquillizers and psychoanalysis.

Chinese physicians realize that illness can be located at the skin, flesh, bone, meridian, or organ levels, and they use terms like superficial, medial and inner to describe this. They also use terms like 'solid illness' for diseases such as a viral attack or a structural defect where the causes are easily discernable; and 'empty illness' for diseases where the causes are not obvious, such as hormone imbalances or functional disorders. So, the next time you and your Western doctor cannot find the cause of your illness, you could seek a second opinion from a Chinese physician to see if your illness is 'empty'.

Should anyone think that Chinese medicine is superstitious or unscientific, he should remind himself that it is the longest lasting continuous medical system known to man, and has been successfully used by the world's largest population, one that has enjoyed very high levels of civilization many times in history. The Chinese successfully treated contagious diseases long before antibiotics were known in the West, performed surgical operations when doctors in the West were content with cupping and blood-letting, and cured emotional and mental illnesses when those in the West thought that such disorders were caused by evil spirits.

But, of course, no one denies the achievements and great contributions of Western medicine. There are many occasions when Western medicine is better than or preferable to Chinese medicine, and on such occasions Chinese physicians do not hesitate to advise their patients to see Western doctors.

Therapeutic Principles of Chi Kung

How does Chinese medical philosophy explain the curing of 'incurable' diseases by practising chi kung? Interestingly, the complex problems concerning the wide range of these diseases that have long puzzled Western medical thinking, can be neatly summarized into two basic principles in chi kung therapy, namely 'harmonizing yin-yang' and 'cleansing meridians'.

Let us take diabetes as illustration. All parts of our body are connected by an intricate network of meridians. When sugar reaches a critical level in the bloodstream, chi or energy flows along a set of meridians, known as yin meridians, to transmit this information to all parts of our body, especially to the 'heart', which, in Chinese medical philosophy often refers not to that tough organ that pumps blood but to the mind or consciousness. The mind sends a flow of chi along another set of meridians, the yang meridians, to all parts of the body, especially the pancreas, to prepare them to meet this situation. The pancreas then produces just the right amount of insulin to neutralize the excessive sugar, and will perfectly adjust the production as the situation requires. This is a natural function, and is possible if the flow of chi along the yin and yang meridians is harmonious, communicating the right information. This condition is expressed as yin-yang harmony.

However, if the chi flow is interrupted, information may be distorted. For example, if some of the yin meridians are blocked some of the chi or energy impulses supplying information may not reach the mind, with the result that the mind thinks there is less sugar than there actually is. As the mind responds according to the information it receives, it will instruct the pancreas to produce less insulin than required. If this disharmony persists, diabetes still occurs even if the patient does not take in much sugar.

Let us say there is no blockage along the yin meridians so that the mind can receive the right information. It will, therefore, send the right instructions to the pancreas. However, if some of the yang meridians are blocked, some of the chi impulses carrying information will not reach the pancreas, resulting in the pancreas receiving wrong information (even though the instructions were correctly given by the mind). Thus the pancreas will produce less insulin than needed. If the yin-yang disharmony is not corrected, diabetes will result.

Injecting insulin into the patient is only treating the symptom. More seriously, though not many people seem to realize its significance, this dependence on injected insulin may make the pancreas so lazy or disused that it may lose its natural ability to produce insulin. Chinese medical philosophy emphasizes treating the cause, not the symptom. As the cause in this example is the malfunction of the pancreas due to blocked meridians, the logical treatment is to cleanse the meridians to restore the pancreas function.

But what causes blocked meridians? 'Blockage' does not necessarily mean that no chi passes through, in which case the patient may die, but means the chi flow is interrupted. Chi blockage may be caused by injury, wrong food, inefficient waste disposal or stress.

A physical blow to a meridian, such as the famous 'death-touch' technique of Shaolin Kungfu, may block its chi flow. Some foods, such as salted vegetables and sour mangoes, may produce 'gases' that affect chi passage. If the toxic waste of our metabolic processes is not disposed of efficiently it may block meridians.

But by far the most serious contributing factor is excessive stress, which produces negative energy and causes chi blockage. Hence, if you are worried, this will produce negative energy that can block the spleen meridian; you will have no appetite for food even though you may be hungry, because the spleen meridian is connected with digestion. Although excessive worrying directly affects the spleen and the stomach meridian systems, it may also cause problems elsewhere because every part of our body is intricately connected by meridians. For example, because the spleen meridian flows into the heart meridian, blockage in the spleen meridian will also weaken the heart.

When we practise chi kung, we stimulate better chi flow. As we take in good cosmic energy to increase our amount of chi, we enhance our chi flow which can push through blockages. This is known as 'breakthrough' in chi kung terminology. The negative, stale chi that blocked the meridians is gradually dispelled out of the body through breathing out, diffusion through the skin, sweating and in other ways. This is known as 'dispelling stale chi and taking in fresh chi'.

As chi circulation is enhanced throughout the body, blockages at other places are also cleared. Hence, enhanced chi flow to cure diabetes can also cure other diseases. This is the holistic aspect of chi kung. If the practitioner continues his chi kung practice, he will not only keep his organs in tip-top condition but also prevent illness from developing in the future.

Life is a Meaningful Exchange of Energy

In the above example, it is assumed that the pancreas is structurally intact, and the disorder is functional. In Chinese medical philosophy, functional disorder is known as yang-illness, in contrast to structural disorder, which is yin-illness.

Prolonged functional disorder will lead to structural disorder. But structural disorder can also be caused by other factors, such as bacterial attack, physical injury or emotional stress. Emotional stress may, figuratively, harden an organ, as the negative energy produced by negative emotions is trapped and congested between and within the organ cells where vital energy is supposed to flow and bathe the cells, bringing nutrients and disposing of toxic waste.

Indeed, all our organs, tissues and cells are exposed to attacks by micro-organisms, wear and tear, all sorts of stress, and many other hazards all the time. It is a wonder of God, or Nature, that we survive all these assaults, because of our wonderful self-defence, self-generative, self-healing and other systems. All these systems will function properly if our vital energy is flowing harmoniously. Actually, the description of the delicate co-operation between the pancreas and other organs in relation to sugar control in our blood stream given on p 125 is similar to the delicate co-operation between all the tissues and cells within the pancreas – except that we have to change the perspective from the system level to the cellular level.

If there are hostile micro-organisms attacking the tissues of the pancreas, energy impulses along yin meridians will inform the mind or relevant control centres, which will send instructions along yang meridians to trigger the defence system to overcome the invaders. If toxic waste products are left in the cells of the pancreas, yin energy impulses will inform the relevant control centres, and yang energy instruction will direct microscopic 'workers' to clear the rubbish away. Life, as defined by many modern biologists, is a meaningful exchange of energy. If the flow of energy is harmonious, described by Chinese medical philosophers as yin-yang harmony, life goes on – structurally, functionally, and in countless other ways.

The principles outlined in this description of diabetes and pancreas function also apply to all other diseases and organs. At all times and in all of us, fat is being deposited in our blood vessels, pollutants are choking our lungs, calcium is forming into stones in our kidneys, acids are pouring into our stomachs, poisons are clogging body and brain cells, yet we do not suffer from hypertension, asthma, kidney stones, peptic ulcers, rheumatism and migraine because our body produces the right types and amounts of chemicals in the right places at the right times. This wonderful natural ability goes on as long as our vital energy is flowing harmoniously.

This may possibly explain why chi kung has been effective in curing many different types of cancer. Western cancer experts have found that everyone has cancer thousands of times during their lifetime, but the body systems overcome it the same number of times without us realizing. Is this because of harmonious chi flow?

14

SAY GOODBYE TO STRESS

Chi Kung for Stress Management and Emotional Stability

❖ *It is well known that chi kung exponents are not only fit and healthy, but also calm and cheerful, even under trying circumstances.*

Chinese Psychology and Psychiatry

How seriously stress affects health is evident from the fact that 'the three most commonly prescribed drugs in the world are all used to combat the destructive effects of stress: an ulcer drug, a drug for hypertension, and Valium (diazepam).'[1] Stress not only causes a wide range of physical and emotional illnesses, but also reduces the efficiency of 'healthy' people in their daily activities.

Chi kung is an excellent way to manage stress. It is well known that chi kung exponents are not only fit and healthy, but also calm and cheerful, even under trying circumstances. This chapter will explain why, and describe how you can be fresh and relaxed.

Practising chi kung not only enables us to say goodbye to stress so that we can work and play better, and relieves sufferers from their stress-related physical and mental disorders, but also promotes emotional stability and inner growth. Physical diseases that are caused by stress, and are often misconceived as incurable, have been dealt with in the previous chapter. Here we shall examine stress-related mental illness and emotional stability.

Many readers may think that psychology and psychiatry were unknown in Chinese medicine, for, as far as I know, almost nothing has been written about these subjects in English.

Actually, Chinese medicine is exceedingly rich in psychology and psychiatry, and Western psychiatrists will benefit much if they care to investigate further. Yet, interestingly enough, psychiatrists never existed as a separate professional group in Chinese medical history! This is because both the Chinese medical profession and the community have never divorced physical and mental illness, for they have always regarded the mind and the body as a unity.

The Chinese also do not make a clear distinction between neurotic and psychiatric disorders, which are generally referred to as illnesses of the 'heart'. In Chinese, the term 'heart' frequently means the mind, and has mental and emotional as well as spiritual dimensions. For our purpose here, such illness of the 'heart' is referred to as emotional illness, for it is often caused by excessive negative emotions.

It is also interesting to note that Chinese physicians generally have not given the brain the special attention that Western doctors often give it as man's central controlling organ. This does not mean they did not know of an organ called a brain. Indeed the Chinese had detailed knowledge of the anatomy and physiology of the brain long before people in the West.

Diseases of the brain and the nervous system are rightly treated in the same way as diseases of other organs. Chinese records show that the great 2nd-century physician, Hua Tuo, performed cranial operations successfully. In his colossal *Causes of Diseases*, the great physician of the 7th century, Chao Yuan Fang, prescribed many chi kung therapeutic exercises to cure diseases of the nervous systems, which the Chinese figuratively described as illnesses caused by 'wind'. In Western medicine, neurology was established as a proper discipline only in the 19th century, and psychiatry many years later.

Chinese physicians do not classify psychiatry as a separate discipline because psychological and psychiatric considerations have always been regarded as essential in all diseases. The *Nei Jing*, or *Inner Classic of Medicine*, repeatedly emphasizes that:

> Mind has not improved,
> Thoughts and feelings not cured,
> The patient will not recover.

As classical Chinese is a very concise language, some scholars often miss the profound wisdom of these classical Chinese works in their translation. The above statement means that:

If a physician considers only the physiological and pathological factors of the patient, neglecting the psychological and psychiatric aspects, the patient will not be cured of his illness.

Dong Jiang Hua and Ma Ming Ren conclude, 'Thus, famous physicians throughout the ages have advocated that those skilful in medicine would first heal the patients' mind, only then heal the patients' body.'[2]

The numerous methods in Chinese medicine to heal the patients' mind can be classified into seven main categories: calming the mind, opening the 'heart' (which will make the patients cheerful), overcoming suspicion, transferring focus, providing convincing explanation, circulating energy, and controlling the interplay of emotions.[3] Chi kung therapy is directly involved in the first and the sixth categories.

Psychoanalysis in Ancient China

The West generally regards Sigmund Freud as the inventor of psychoanalysis. However, psychoanalysis was practised in ancient China, the difference being that, unlike Freud, Chinese physicians did not place special importance on the sex complex.

A mandarin in ancient China named Zhang Jing Quan frequently dreamed that a man in a white robe would cut off his head. He also had this vision whenever he closed his eyes to meditate. No medicine could cure him, making him severely depressed, until he consulted the famous physician Shen Lu Zhen. After a thorough examination, the physician said authoritatively, 'Isn't it stated in the *Nei Jing* that white symbolizes the lungs, and that if internal organs are weak, the patient would dream of being beheaded? Your symptoms and your dreams show that your lungs are weak. Great masters have recorded that such a sickness can easily be cured by taking white ginseng.' As the mandarin was well read in medical literature too, the physician often had discussions with him and explained to him the finer points of Chinese medicine. Soon the mandarin's emotional illness was cured.

Other physicians had also diagnosed the same cause and prescribed the same medication. Why then were they not successful in curing the mandarin? It was because they treated only his body, and neglected his mind. Shen Lu Zhen effectively removed the mandarin's emotional problem by convincing him that his nightmare was merely a symptom of his illness, and then further reaffirmed the patient's confidence in him by his masterful discussion of medical matters. It is interesting to note the parallel observation by modern doctors that patients with heart problems often dream of falling from great heights, and tuberculosis patients dream of shouldering heavy burdens.[4]

While phobia was not recognized by Western medicine as a particular sickness until the 19th century, it was defined and effectively treated in ancient China. During the first century the prince of Chu had a peculiar illness. He could not sleep, had an irrational fear of meeting people, and was even frightened of people's voices. His court physicians were puzzled. At last they consulted Wu Rong Jie. After a detailed diagnosis, the physician told the prince that he suffered from 'the sickness of fear', which could not be treated by oral medication nor acupuncture, but could be cured by long discussion over a long time.

The physician advised the prince, 'Your Highness could start by listening to harmonious music, because music can clear the chi of our heart and lungs. You must also take delicious food which is fragrant and well decorated, and which will also delight your invited guests. Once in a while you should ride a good horse far out into the wilderness and enjoy the unlimited expanse of open sky and pure, fresh air. You may also bring along your bow and arrows and hunt some wild animals. The fun of eating barbecued meat hunted by you cannot be described in words.' Soon the prince changed his lifestyle and 'opened' his heart. Without his being aware of it, his phobia gradually disappeared.[5]

Flushing Out Negative Emotions

What has chi kung to do with all these psychiatric problems? Everything, because emotional disorders are caused by disharmony of chi. Chinese medical philosophers classify the causes of illness into three groups: 'six evils of external causes', 'seven emotions of internal causes' and 'neither-internal-nor-external causes'. The seven emotions, which are principally responsible for emotional illness, are joy, anger, anxiety, worry, sorrow, fear and shock.

According to Chinese medical thought, lack of joy injures the heart, anger injures the liver, anxiety and sorrow injure the lungs, worry injures the spleen, fear and shock injure the kidneys. When a person is joyful, his energy flows well; but excessive joy or lack of joy would cause his chi to disperse. When a person is angry, his chi rushes to his head. Anxiety causes chi flow to be sluggish; whereas worry makes chi clot. Sorrow weakens chi and drains it away. Fear causes chi to sink, while shock causes chi to be confused.

Translated into simple language, it means that if you are cheerful, illness is unlikely to visit you. A sorrowful person tends to have weak lungs, and is prone to diseases like bronchitis and tuberculosis, while one who is easily angered increases his chance of having hypertension and heart diseases. Anxious, worried people usually have illnesses of the digestive system; whereas severe fright may cause a person to urinate without control.

As all these organs are closely linked to the 'heart', which means the mind in Chinese medicine, prolonged disharmonious chi will cause not only organic diseases associated with the respective organs, but also emotional ailments, that is, psychological disorders. For example, excessive sorrow may weaken a person's chi so much that its flow to his mind may become insufficient to operate certain mental functions, resulting in depression, insanity and other psychiatric problems. The chi flow may be inadequate to dispose of toxic waste in the brain, resulting in neurological disorders.

The best way to overcome this disharmony of chi is to practise chi kung, which remedies the disorders at both levels, that is, it increases the amount of chi as well as effecting smooth chi flow.

Negative emotions are brought about internally. Depending on the different levels of chi harmony in different people, the same situation may generate a negative emotion in one, but not in another, or may affect the same person in different ways at different times.

The loss of money or reputation, for example, may be very stressful to some people, producing negative energy that becomes blocked in meridians, and may seriously affect their physical or psychological well-being. To a chi kung practitioner, because his chi flow is harmonious, the same loss may not affect his health as much, as the negative energy produced is readily flushed out. Many people become furious or anxious when caught in traffic jams because of the pent up negative energy produced, even though they realize that the resultant negative emotions cannot enable them to reach their destination faster. In similar situations, chi kung practitioners can remain calm because their energy flows smoothly.

As we progress in chi kung training, our amount of chi increases, and our chi flow becomes smoother. Hence, in addition to the other benefits, we become emotionally stable and strong, and able to tolerate anxiety, annoyance, grievance, aggression and other emotional stress that other people would succumb to.

Stress Management and Emotional Stability

Stress occurs when energy is blocked. Once released, this energy can be put to useful work. Chi kung is an excellent system to achieve this.

One of the first things a chi kung student learns is how to relax both physically and mentally. If you have been practising the chi kung exercises explained in the previous chapters correctly, you will have said goodbye to stress by now.

The following is another simple yet effective method to manage stress.

Stand, sit or lie down comfortably. Close your eyes and smile from your heart.

Starting from the top of your head relax all parts of your body, slowly working down your trunk, arms and legs, right to your toes. A rough guideline for the time taken to feel relaxation from head to toes is about five minutes; but you can perform the procedure faster or slower as your need requires.

Next, using your normal method of breathing and without paying much attention to it, breathe slowly and gently about ten times. Then forget about your breathing, forget about yourself, forget about everything for five to ten minutes — but gently remind yourself not to fall asleep.

Complete the exercise by warming your eyes and massaging your face as usual. Feel how fresh and relaxed you are.

You should not be disturbed in the midst of your practice. The precautions and remedies explained in Chapter 11, p 101, will be helpful if you need them.

The Psychological Aspects of Chi Kung

Managing stress, though very important and very beneficial to many people, is only an elementary achievement in chi kung – an ability that all chi kung students are expected to attain. Yet, if you continue to practise the comparatively elementary exercise described above over a long period, you may one day derive effects that may astound you. This exemplifies one remarkable feature of chi kung; the technique that ultimately produces fantastic results, often thought of by lay people as advanced and elaborated, is often very simple! The key lies not in the technique, but in years of consistent training.

Anybody who feels stressed can practise the simple relaxation exercise described above for about ten minutes with obvious benefits. If he practises it daily, he can efficiently prevent emotional disorders. Those with psychiatric problems are advised to consult a psychiatrist, chi kung therapist or other professional healer. However, if they wish to try chi kung exercises to overcome their emotional disorders, either as the main or a supplementary therapeutic method, it is recommended that they also include Induced Chi Flow (Chapter 7), Abdominal Breathing (Chapter 9), and later, only when they are more stable, meditation (Chapter 10).

Chi kung not only cures and prevents emotional illness, it also promotes emotional development and mental performance. Wang Ji Sheng, one of modern China's foremost psychologists who has done much research, and who is also a chi kung master, reports:

Preliminary results of chi kung research show that practising chi kung consistently definitely improves and increases people's memory, reasoning ability, concentration power and voluntary movements.[6]

China has experienced an unprecedented period of rapid industrialization since the founding of the Chinese Peoples' Republic. The traditional way of life has been revolutionized and the people are exposed to tremendous stress, yet Chinese society does not face the serious psychiatric problems common to other industrial countries. Wang Ji Sheng suggests that this is due to the fact that a large proportion of the Chinese population practises chi kung daily.

The noted psychologist adds:

> Through systematic research in chi kung, from the perspective of understanding the levels and opening of man's intelligence and mental potential, we may achieve a breakthrough in this area ... It is likely that around the year 2000, the psychological and health aspects found in chi kung may develop to become a special feature of the psychology and health science of the Chinese people.[7]

Wang Ji Sheng emphasizes that one can find in chi kung much profound material concerning psychology. He classifies psychological material in chi kung into the following 11 areas, which also correspond to the principles found in ancient Chinese arts of health and longevity.[8]

1 Unity of consciousness and body.
2 Unity of jing, chi and shen – essence, energy and mind.
3 Spirit as the real controller of life.
4 Emphasis on mind, rather than body, in the promotion of health and longevity.
5 Emphasis on morality in mind training.
6 Importance of mind, in the training to attain 'harmonies of mind, of breathing and of posture'.
7 Function of mind in the 'cultivation of silence'.
8 Mind training according to time and seasons.
9 Seven emotions as internal causes of illness.
10 Pain as a symptom of energy blockage.
11 Different levels of consciousness in meditation.

Chi kung, therefore, is not just a set of gentle exercises or a system of breathing techniques, as many people, including chi kung students, mistakenly believe. Among other things, chi kung has much to contribute to health and medicine, providing a comprehensive theory and practice for curing so-called incurable diseases, and relieving psychological disorders without the use of drugs. For those of you who are lucky not to be troubled by such medical problems, but who are looking for more energy and stamina for sports and games, the next chapter will show you how to use chi kung to become champions.

15

ENERGY AND STAMINA FOR CHAMPIONS

Chi Kung for Sportsmen and Martial Artists

❖ *It is a mistake to think that it is only Chinese athletes who use chi kung exclusively in their training.*

The Secret of Champions

One striking feature of international sports is the emergence of China as a leading nation within a comparatively short time. Less than 50 years ago, China was unknown in the international arena, but now the Chinese not only excel in games such as table tennis and badminton, but also have broken world records in events where their relatively small size is a disadvantage, such as in high jump and weightlifting. The secret is chi kung, and the following facts provide an illuminating picture.

The earliest modern Chinese athlete of international fame who categorically attributed his success to chi kung training was Mu Xiang Xiong, who broke the world swimming record for 100 metre breaststroke three times in 1958 and 1959. His training methods would astound many readers. He spent much of his time not in the water perfecting his strokes, but on land, practising the horseriding stance, deep breathing and meditation – the basic training, he explained, that won him the world titles.[1]

After confirming the effective role of chi kung in sports, in 1978 the Chinese National Sports Council instructed selected sport colleges to include chi kung in their training.[2] Now every Chinese national team in whatever sport or game must have the

Fig 15.1   Horse-Riding Stance

services of at least one chi kung master. The master not only teaches the sportsmen relevant chi kung techniques, but also speeds up their recovery from injuries by transmitting chi to them.

Bei Jia Te and his colleagues, who were involved in using chi kung to train national athletes, reported that there was a remarkable difference in both the improvement in physiological function and actual performance between sportsmen with chi kung training and control groups who had no chi kung training. For example, in the summer training of 1980, the chi kung group improved noticeably in all the five events of 100 metres, 400 metres, high jump, long jump and shot put; whereas for the control groups there was a slight improvement in the 100 metres and 400 metres events, but their performance deteriorated in the other three events. In another programme, a basketball player improved his jump from 1.65 metres to 1.85 metres after chi kung practice, without any jumping practice. Another athlete improved his performance in the 5,000 metres and 1,500 metres events, from 15 minutes 36 seconds and 4 minutes 13 seconds, to 15 minutes 22 seconds and 4 minutes 6 seconds respectively, with chi kung training only. In the 5,000 metres, he broke the Hupei provincial record for the first 3,000 metres. The fact that he did it just by practising chi kung, and without any specialized training in running is incredible.[3]

It is a mistake to think that it is only Chinese athletes who use chi kung extensively in their training. In the Asian Games held in Seoul, the host country, South Korea, won a lot of gold medals. When foreign reporters visited their sport village to discover the secret of their success, they were surprised that the secret was chi kung. For instance, Kim Chan Hao, who had won two world gold medals for archery, practised meditation daily.[4]

Chi kung techniques, known by other names, are practised widely by many world athletes. Carl Lewis, the American who won the 100 metres in the 1984 Olympics, explained:

> In the first 50 metres I ran very fast. Then I gradually relaxed my muscles. The more you relax, the more slowly will your speed be reduced. Hence, from 70 metres till the finishing point, I was much faster than anybody.[5]

At present, competition in international sports has become so close that the decisive factor is often not technical skill or physical prowess, but mental concentration, determination and confidence. Because many sportsmen emphasize only technique, stamina and endurance, they fail to perform their best in important competitions, though they do well during practice. Hence, experts in sports are now placing more and more importance on training the mind as well as the body. Mind training, incorporating features like concentration, determination and confidence, can be effectively realized in chi kung.

Chi Kung in Martial Arts

Chi kung is equally, if not more, important in martial arts. In some martial arts like Shaolin Kungfu, Tai Chi Chuan and Aikido, an understanding and development of chi is essential for those who wish to progress to the advanced level.

Many people wonder why traditional kungfu masters of Southern Shaolin asked their students to spend months practising the horse-riding stance before learning any kungfu techniques. In addition to building a solid foundation for footwork, the horse-riding stance develops and stores chi at the energy field at the abdomen, called dan tian, so that later the vital energy can be channelled as internal force to where it is desired. This reservoir of chi at the dan tian is the fountainhead of internal force, enabling kungfu masters to accomplish fantastic feats such as injuring an opponent without leaving any external mark, or fighting for many hours without feeling breathless. In Northern Shaolin, proper breath control is necessary for agility, speed, and various kicking techniques.

Have you ever wondered why Tai Chi Chuan (Taijiquan), the 'soft' style of Chinese martial art that is popular throughout the world, is usually practised slowly and gracefully, yet Tai Chi Chuan masters can marshal tremendous power with their seemingly gentle movements? The answer lies in chi kung. Without understanding and developing chi, it is simply impossible to train the internal force which gives Tai Chi Chuan its well-known combat efficiency. Even if one practices Tai Chi Chuan for health, and not for fighting, without developing chi, the essence of its health promotion is inevitably lost; it degrades into a form of gentle dance! Performing the movements slowly is one effective way to train chi, which can manifest into tremendous power without being rough or brutal.

'Aikido' means 'the way of chi harmony'. The Aikido master, Koichi Tohei, is well known for his unbendable arm, which cannot be moved even by a strong person. He explains that this is possible when he visualizes chi (called 'ki' in Japanese) flowing endlessly through his arm, making it like a powerful waterhose.

Circulating Hands for Power

There are four main areas where chi kung is very useful to sportsmen and martial artists, namely in increasing power, improving stamina, enhancing split-second decision making and aiding recovery from injury.

Power is an essential ingredient for success in any sport or martial art. If your tennis smash or karate strike, for example, is not powerful, you are not likely to beat your opponent, even though your technique may be better. Many years ago, a group of kungfu exponents from Hong Kong were badly beaten in the ring by professional Siamese boxers. As well as having no previous fighting experience, these mercenary Kungfu exponents had no power in attack or in defence. They could not withstand even a single powerful kick from the Siamese boxers.

The way Siamese boxers train to develop their powerful kicks, is similar to the 'hard chi kung' training in Shaolin Kungfu, where the student kicks at sandbags, poles or tree trunks hundreds of times a day for many months if not years. There is no secret technique; it is sheer hard work. After kicking at sandbags millions of times, your kicks will naturally be powerful, fluid and fast.

However, if you are not ready to endure such demanding training, there are other more gentle ways. A Tai Chi Chuan or an Aikido master, for example, may have never struck a sandbag or a pole in his training, but his strike is as forceful as a Siamese boxer's kick. Their training is by way of chi, which, as well as needing much time and effort, also requires appropriate techniques. One useful technique is called Circulating Hands.

Start by practising Abdominal Breathing about 36 times to store vital energy at your abdominal dan tian. Then stand at the goat-riding stance, and with your palms open and facing inward, gently circulate both hands in front of your body, with your left hand moving anti-clockwise, and your right hand moving clockwise, Figure 15.2. Continue your abdominal breathing, without any need to co-ordinate your breathing with your hand movements, but visualize your cosmic energy flowing into your abdomen as you breathe in, and vital energy flowing from your abdomen to your arms as you breathe out. Practise for about 15 to 30 minutes a day for at least six months.

Fig 15.2   Circulating Hands

This Circulating Hands exercise does not only circulate energy to the hands, nor does it benefit only martial artists. Because all parts of the body are connected by an intricate network of meridians, energy will be circulated throughout the body, bringing nutrients to every cell and taking toxic waste away. If you practise Circulating Hands you will find you have more power in any sport or game you take part in.

Breath Co-ordination for Stamina

Stamina is an important factor for success in any sport or martial art. Many years ago, I saw some kungfu sparring competitions where many competitors were panting heavily after the second round. Some could not even lift up their hands, and they blamed their defeat on the gloves they wore, which they claimed restricted their kungfu techniques, forgetting that even with the gloves on a kungfu exponent has a greater range of techniques to use than a karate or taekwondo exponent would. The reason was not a lack of technique, but a lack of power and stamina. When your opponent no longer has strength to carry on, if you still have striking power and stamina you need only walk in and fell him with one forceful blow, even though that blow may be very unartistic and technically inferior. This applies as much to sports and games as to martial arts.

The secret of stamina is continuously to replenish energy before it is used up. For untrained persons, when their movements become fast or vigorous, their breathing also speeds up to increase the intake of cosmic energy or air to meet the extra demand. Hence they pant for breath, and if they cannot replenish their energy adequately, they become short of breath.

Chi kung is an excellent way to overcome this problem for athletes, martial artists and all other people. Three factors are involved: keeping an adequate reserve of energy, having smooth pathways of energy flow from the reserve to where energy is needed, and replenishing the reserve efficiently. In the past, kungfu masters who had achieved the breakthrough of the Small Universe where their vital energy flowed in a never-ending circle round their ren and du meridians, could fight for hours without becoming breathless. The Small Universe is an advanced chi kung technique that needs a master's supervision during training. Nevertheless, the following easier method will meet the needs of most people.

First you need to be familiar with Abdominal Breathing (p 76) which enables you to reserve energy at your abdominal energy field. Secondly, you must have regularly performed induced chi flow or other appropriate chi kung exercises so that your meridians are clear for smooth energy flow. Then you must practise the following breath co-ordination exercise so that, despite fast or vigorous movements, you can maintain slow, deep breathing to replenish energy efficiently.

> During your martial art training or sport practice, take a deep breath slowly through your nose into your abdominal energy field. Gently hold your breath, but have your lips slightly open so that any breath needing to go out can flow out gently on its own, without your conscious effort. Simultaneously, continue your sport or martial art movements. When you feel that you have used up about 70 per cent of the energy in your abdominal energy field, take in another deep breath slowly. Continue this process.

In this way, you will always have about 30 per cent of energy reserved in your abdomen, and you will always breathe in slowly and deeply, though your movements may be fast. Instead of consciously breathing out, you gently hold your breath, but you allow any breath to flow out on its own if it becomes too compressed.

Be moderate in your training. Initially, do not move too fast, nor have too many movements for one breath. This means that at the beginning your performance may be worse than your normal standard, because you have not only to concentrate on your breathing, but also intentionally to slow down your movements for better co-ordination. But as you progress in the training, your speed will naturally increase, and when you are familiar with the technique, it becomes second nature without any conscious effort. Your friends will be surprised at how you can last so long or perform so fast in sports or martial arts. Of course, as in any art, you need to put in a lot of time and effort before you become competent in the technique.

The Importance of Mind

At the amateur level, power and stamina, as well as technique, make a lot of difference to someone's performance in sports and martial art. But at the professional level, it is often the mind that becomes the most important decisive factor in the making of champions.

Four aspects of mind function affect our sport and martial art performance: relaxation, concentration, decision-making, and visualization.

To be able to relax physically and mentally is a crucial factor in any sport or martial art. We may be very skilful and know a lot of effective techniques, but if we become wrought up or tensed when facing an opponent, we perform 'out of form'. To be calm and relaxed is a basic feature we acquire from chi kung training.

While we are relaxed, we must also be able to concentrate intensely on our performance, even to the extent of forgetting everything else. Readers who think that relaxing and concentrating at the same time is a contradiction, illustrate the limitations of language. We certainly can do this; in fact, this is what an important aspect of meditation is about. In chi kung we develop our mind to be one-pointed, so that whether we are shooting a football into a goal, or warding off a thrust from a fencing opponent, we will be able to give our best performance because our mind is both calm and focused.

Making the right split-second decisions is crucial to sport and martial art success. In the past it might have meant life or death to kungfu fighters. When our mind is calm and focused, we certainly can think more clearly. If we attain a deeper level of consciousness, we may even transcend time! Years ago, when I used to spar frequently with martial artists, I had some interesting experiences. At times, as a sparring partner attacked me, an array of possible counters flashed across my mind, allowing me to debate which counter was best for that particular situation. The attack happened in a split second, but in my meditative state, it appeared to be a minute, hence giving me sufficient time to decide. I guess many sportsmen will have had similar experiences, when, in a meditative state of mind, time seemed to slow down for them, allowing them time to make just the right decision. Chi kung training is one possible way to prepare for such an experience.

A very useful meditation technique for sportsmen and martial artists who aim to be champions, is visualization. Before you can apply this technique effectively, you must have attained a meditative level in which you can keep your mind focused on one object or on the void for some time. In your meditation, visualize the beautiful, masterful movements you dream of executing in your sport; a perfect stroke in golf or a faultless throw in judo, for example. Go over these champion's strokes a few times in your mind so that they are immersed in your subconscious. You must practise this meditation technique gently; there must never be any stress whatsoever on your mind. When taking part in your sport, especially when a situation similar to that in your meditation occurs, execute the strokes just as you visualized them.

Chi Kung for Speedy Recovery

Sustaining injury is an unfortunate feature of competitive sports and martial arts. Speedy recovery is certainly a great advantage, especially when a series of competitions is spread over many days. As I was brought up in a traditional kungfu environment, where the master usually knew Chinese medicine and students were always given medical treatment for any injury sustained, I was very surprised when students of other martial arts told me that whenever they sustained injury, their instructors merely asked them to bend their body many times or jump about to dissipate the injury! If an injury is not cured, it may cause serious problems in later life. In kungfu training, external injury is often treated by applying medicinal wine, and internal injury by taking herbal concoctions.

A more effective, more convenient and faster way is chi kung therapy, which can be performed by a master or by the sportsman himself. An effective method of self-healing using chi kung is to perform Lifting the Sky about ten times, breathing in gently, but breathing out speedily and forcefully. Continue with induced chi flow, gently visualizing vital energy cleansing and curing your injury. You may feel some pain as the internal chi flow works on your injury. Then go into meditation, preferably sitting meditation, experiencing the beautiful process of self-healing, and later the state of being healed.

To some people unfamiliar with chi kung and other esoteric arts, self-healing through meditation or perfecting techniques through visualization may sound bizarre. But, in line with Shaolin philosophy, readers are requested not to accept anything in this book on faith alone, but are invited to try the suggested techniques with an open mind and then evaluate them according to their own experience. Of course, if it takes you a few months to perfect a basketball throw or a swimming stroke, it is reasonable to require at least a few months of practice with such 'intangible' things as energy and mind. Our mind is wonderful, and you will read more about its wonders in the next chapter.

REACHING FOR THE REMARKABLE AND THE DIVINE

Chi Kung to Enhance Mental Performance

❖ *Our personal mind becomes united with the Universal Mind, enabling us to experience the undifferentiated, non-dualistic Supreme Reality.*

The Wonderful Mind

Roger was a PhD student. He had some problems with his doctorate thesis. He discussed the problems with his friends and with his supervisor, read all the relevant books he could find, stretched his conscious mind to its limit, viewed his problems from many angles, yet he could not solve his problems. So he went into meditation and posed the problems to his subconscious mind. He did this a few times. Then one day, as soon as he posed his problems, the answers flashed across his mind. 'The solutions are so simple,' he said, 'it was astonishing no one thought of them in this way before.'

Aminah had some cracks in her eardrum. Her specialist doctors told her that she must go for an ear operation to get the cracks stitched or they would become bigger and bigger and she might become deaf. She sought my advice when I visited her chi kung class one night. I asked her whether she could delay the operation for six months. She consulted her doctors, who told her that although there was no immediate threat to life, it was better to have the operation early as there was no other way her eardrum could be cured.

I taught Aminah how to channel her chi to her eardrum, and how to visualize during meditation to heal the cracks. When she consulted her ear specialist three months later, he was surprised that the cracks were healing, a phenomenon he had never heard of before. Six months later, after giving her a thorough examination, the specialist told Aminah the operation was not necessary for her eardrum was cured!

Veronica was a renowned pianist. Yet there were some musical complexities she could not master. One evening, after meditating, she told me excitedly, 'Sifu, I saw my mind!' 'How do you know it was your mind?' I asked. 'I don't know the reasons, but I know it was my mind. I just know,' she replied confidently. 'What did you see in your mind?' 'Those musical complexities that have troubled me for years. You know what happened? The complexities became so easy.'

I left Veronica on her own to try out her musical complexities. A few days later she told me gratefully, 'Your chi kung meditation has helped me to solve my musical complexities which all my music lessons and music teachers could not solve for 20 years. Thank you very much, Sifu.'

Soon Veronica had to prepare for a continental tour for her piano recitals. She requested me to transmit chi to her (over 5,000km) to help her in her public performances, which were crucial to her career. I taught her to visualize in her deep meditation scenes that she would like to happen in her performances. She wrote back later telling me she had had many standing ovations, almost exactly as she had visualized!

It was a warm spring night in Australia. Belinda, a pious Christian, sat cross-legged on a hard pillow on the floor with her eyes closed. In her meditation, I led her into a deep level of her consciousness. Suddenly she cried. I comforted her, assured her that everything would be all right, and asked her her name. 'Maria,' she murmured. 'Why are you so sad, Maria?' 'They killed my father. We've lost everything.' 'Who killed your father?' 'The Roundheads.' 'What period is it now?' 'The 1640s,' she said, and continued to describe happenings of the English Civil War. Seeing that she felt miserable, I led her to another epoch of her past lives, but when she spoke again she was still the same Maria, though many years later. She told us she was a governess, and she described her surroundings, which we interpreted as a medieval castle. 'It's cold, very cold.' 'Why is it cold?' 'It's winter and there's no fire.'

When Belinda came out of her meditation, she said she knew exactly what had transpired. She was a bit embarrassed about the crying, but said it gave her a wonderful cathartic effect. 'But I'm not cold now,' she added. The interesting thing was that both she and her husband, who was with us throughout her past-life regression session, knew little about the English Civil War. The next day her husband borrowed some relevant books from the local library, and they were amazed that all the happenings Maria had described were correct. 'Thank you very much for this extraordinary experience, Sifu,' Belinda concluded. 'It enables me to understand myself better.'

Many readers may find these case histories incredible. I know they are true because they happened to people who learned chi kung from me or from my disciples, and I was involved in three of the cases.

Different Levels of Consciousness

Incredible feats are known as special extraordinary abilities in chi kung. They were regarded as miraculous powers in the past. They are neither occult nor supernatural, though they are certainly not easily understood by ordinary people. These special extraordinary abilities can be acquired by those who have attained an advanced level in chi kung.

How does advanced chi kung enable us to acquire special extraordinary abilities? The most important factor is meditation, or mind training, to attain different levels of consciousness. These abilities are amply explained in classical chi kung literature.

In describing advanced chi kung concepts, certain terms that are commonly found in Taoist and Buddhist literature, like 'shen' (spirit) and 'xin' (heart or mind), are frequently used. It must be emphasized again that chi kung is definitely non-religious, and the use of such terms is for convenience. It would be extremely clumsy and circumlocutory to replace these useful, concise terms with phrases or clauses. Actually, these terms are philosophical rather than religious in significance: for example, a Christian priest is known in Chinese as 'shen-fu', literally 'a father in (the Christian) religion'.

In Taoist chi kung terminology, the advanced stage of chi kung attainment is called 'training of the spirit to return to the cosmos'. It means that our spirit is so pure and well developed that we, in our spirit, have liberated ourselves from our personal, individualized limitations and that we are no longer restricted by the everyday constructs of time and space. This is the Taoist attainment of immortality! But long before this spiritual fulfilment, the adept would have developed many special extraordinary abilities.

In Buddhist chi kung terminology, this is the transcending of the four levels of 'chan' or 'dhyana' (meditative states), whereby the meditator arrives at the 'alaya consciousness', which is the interface between the personal mind and the 'Yi Xin' or Universal Mind. As his mind has been purified from all defilements, he now sees 'his face before he was born', which is 'the original face of Reality'. He therefore liberates himself from his personal attachment, and attains enlightenment. But long before this state of supreme awareness, he has developed special extraordinary abilities, which are often called 'the six classes of miracles' in Buddhist literature.

Meditation is used in other great religions to attain a union with God. Numerous records of Christian saints show their ecstatic experience of God during meditation or 'orison'. In his meditation, the Christian saint also experiences the expansion of his soul into the cosmos. Marina de Escobar said, 'the soul is then plunged, as it were, into a vast ocean which is God and again God'.[1] The Bible explains, 'There is one God and Father of all mankind, who is Lord of all, works through all, and is in all'.[2]

So, in orison, when the devotee is in God and God is in him, and when God is all, this spiritual experience can be described in other words like the spirit returning to the cosmos, or the individual mind totally immersed in the Universal Mind.

Muslim saints also record similar spiritual experiences during meditation or 'muraqaba'. Dr Mir Valiuddin says the Muslim seeker meditates that 'Grace is flowing over my heart from the Eternal Essence that is with us, and with all our *latifas* [faculties], and with each and every hair of our body, and with each and every particle of the world that encompasseth all things'.[3] Notice how similar to chi kung meditation this method is. After purifying the self and cleansing the heart, the finite is connected to the infinite by muraqaba, which is meditation, whereby the adept attains a state where 'the seeker does not exist, God is all'.[4]

In simple language, and in simplified prosaic terms, the various spiritual experiences show that when we reach very deep levels of consciousness we perceive different levels of reality, with the result that we can transcend time and space! Our personal mind becomes united with the Universal Mind, enabling us to experience the undifferentiated, non-dualistic Supreme Reality. The miracles performed by saints of various religions recorded in history were the result of the attainment of this very deep level of consciousness.

The latest discoveries (rediscoveries?) of modern science confirm what the ancient great masters have always taught. When nuclear physicists look into the very core of matter, as revealed by their sophisticated bubble chambers where sub-atomic particles are studied, they find nothing solid; what they find is undifferentiated energy. In other words, at the subatomic level, the skin that we think separates us from our surroundings does not exist! There is no demarcation line – what we think is the outermost limit of our body is merely a linear concentration of subatomic particles constantly exchanging energy with the so-called external environment. This poetic realization that the whole cosmos is one continuous entity is probably the greatest discovery of modern science.

This is where science and religion meet. Great teachers of different religions have taught that the universe is a living, undifferentiated, organic unity – immanent, omniscient, omnipotent and omnipresent. Because of their cultural and linguistic differences, different peoples have named it in various ways – such as Supreme Reality, Absolute Being, Universal Mind, Brahman, Tao, Tathagata, God. When we experience – not merely understand – this Supreme Reality, we attain the fulfilment of all religions.

Nevertheless, religious fulfilment, though it is the supreme accomplishment of the highest chi kung, is not the main concern of this book or of this chapter. Those who wish to pursue this noble, sacred path – the greatest path any person can ever attempt, if he is ready – will have to follow their own chosen religious ways. What follows is a description of some useful methods to accomplish earthly goals, for example, how chi kung can help business and professional people to solve technical problems, or artists and scientists to produce their great works.

Meditation Technique for Solving Problems

Suppose you are a managing director planning a new strategy for your new product. Three senior executives have presented three different strategies, and as they are equally attractive you have difficulty deciding which one to implement. You wish to apply chi kung meditation to your problem.

First, you need to list your priorities. What are your general aims and specific objectives? Are you more concerned with fulfilling the company's aim, perhaps oftener stated than implemented, of providing better service or goods to the community, or the immediate objective of making more profit for yourself and the company? It is interesting that almost always the less you emphasize your personal interest, the more successful your chosen strategy will be. The reason is not just idealistic altruism, but practical considerations, for when your strategy is targeted for the benefit of most people, you are likely to meet the least resistance.

This does not imply that you should be discouraged from making honest money. Unless you are running a charity, if there is no personal or company interest, there will probably be no problem in the first place. But, even if the meditation technique provides you with an excellent strategy, if it goes against the legitimate interests of many people, inevitable cosmic forces created by thoughts of other people, will be at work and will negate the effects of your otherwise successful strategy. This is not moralizing, but a statement of a basic cosmic law.

When you have a clear concept of your priorities, go into meditation, using one of the methods described in Chapter 10 or any other method you are competent in. It is better to meditate in the single or double lotus position, but if your legs are not flexible enough to sit comfortably in this position, use the simplified sitting upright position.

When you are at 'a chi kung state of mind', which is your subconscious level, that is, when surrounding noises or events do not bother you at all, gently but firmly ask your subconscious mind to show you the best of the three strategies to follow. Do not think, and do not reason, but expect your subconscious mind to give you a clear answer.

Your answer may come immediately, or it may come later

in the same meditation or in another meditation. Or it may come when you are relaxing and least expecting it, for example, when you are playing golf or lying beside a pool. Sometimes your answer may be symbolic, and you will need to interpret the symbols. At times your subconscious may make changes to your original strategy, which you may find surprising, but as the subconscious has access to information often not available to the conscious mind, these changes usually turn out to be very helpful.

Meditation Technique for Creativity

Let us say that you are a novelist dreaming of writing a masterpiece. You cannot just go into meditation and ask your subconscious mind for a novel and expect to get a best-seller. If you try this, you will still get an answer but it will not be satisfactory.

In some ways, your subconscious mind is like a super computer, except it is many, many times more efficient and wonderful. You need to feed your subconscious with the necessary information, such as the type of novel you wish to write, the market you aim to reach and the special effects you hope to create. You will have to do a lot of homework with your conscious mind before you are ready to apply your subconscious.

You can use the chi kung state of mind to feed the required background information to your subconscious. Apply any suitable method to go into meditation. When you are at the chi kung state of mind, which is your subconscious level, meditate on your background information, one piece at a time. For example, repeat silently a few times to yourself while you are in meditation, 'I want to write an excellent novel on the theme, "the pains and joys of growing up" for children between the ages of 15 and 20.' Let the suggestion sink into your subconscious mind.

If you have not consciously thought out the plot of the novel, you can ask your subconscious to supply one in another meditation. If you already have a plot, you can tell your subconscious mind about it, and ask for its comment.

In the same way, you can seek the aid of your subconscious mind for all other aspects of the novel.

When you have become familiar with working at your subconscious level, you do not even have to go into formal meditation to feed data into, or receive ideas from your subconscious mind. Because you have felt so strongly and thought so deeply about your project, it will subconsciously sink into your mind, and helpful ideas will often filter through from your subconscious to your conscious level at odd moments.

On the other hand, if you have a problem, and are undecided as to where or how to obtain help, you can purposely go into meditation and send a signal of your requirement into the cosmos. If you are sincere and meditate deeply enough, your signal will reach the right destination. The principle of 'least self-interest, most likely to succeed' mentioned in the previous application, applies as well here as elsewhere.

For example, you have now written an excellent novel but are undecided as to which publisher to send your manuscript to. If, in your meditation, you instruct your subconscious to enable you to present your manuscript in such a persuasive way that whoever you submit your manuscript to will accept it, you may succeed; but if the published book is not suitable for that publisher it may not sell well, and both you and the publisher will suffer.

But if in your meditation your aim is to find the publisher who will benefit most from your book, you will usually get what you ask for. This publisher will make a lot of money selling your book, but of course you too will be amply rewarded.

These meditation techniques illustrate how we can apply our subconscious mind to solve problems and produce better work. Many modern psychologists and parapsychologists are beginning to accept what ancient masters taught long ago, that is, that thoughts are real things, and we are responsible for our thoughts. History has shown without any doubt that evil thoughts always generate evil energy that inevitably harms the mind that produces it, and sometimes even manifests outwardly to distort the face. So, for our sake as well as others', let us always fill our mind with thoughts that are cheerful and good.

17

TO EACH ACCORDING TO HIS NEEDS

How to Plan Your Own Chi Kung Programme

❖ *Chi kung has great flexibility, enabling it to suit many different needs, and once we know some basic principles it is easy to plan our training programmes according to our needs.*

Planning Chi Kung Programmes

A good chi kung book does not merely provide readers with sound knowledge and useful exercises, but also inspires them and shows them the way so that they can continue to train and become masters themselves. In addition to high moral values, three factors are necessary for someone to become a master: a clear understanding of aims and objectives so that training is directed and time-effective, an ability to handle unintentional injury caused by deviation, and the confidence to modify or plan course material for the individual needs of students. The first two factors have been discussed; we shall examine the third factor in this chapter.

Many students stick rigidly to their teachers' programmes because they are afraid that deviation may cause serious injury. Beginners should follow their teachers' instructions carefully and exactly. However, when they are familiar with the art, it may be helpful to modify their training programmes to suit special situations, provided they fully understand what they are doing and are able to practise remedial exercises should things go wrong. Indeed, chi kung has great flexibility, enabling it to suit many different needs, and once we know some basic principles it is easy to plan our training programmes according to our needs.

We shall use the basic exercises presented in this book as the repertoire from which to devise various training programmes to meet different requirements. Thus, those who are still not familiar with these exercises should read the relevant pages again if they wish to understand clearly what is described below. After studying the examples, readers should be able to devise their own programmes for their own needs.

Shaolin Cosmos Chi Kung

With the exception of the various chi kung types discussed in Chapter 12, the type of chi kung presented in this book is called Shaolin Cosmos Chi Kung – 'Shaolin' because it originated from the Shaolin Monastery, and 'Cosmos' because energy is tapped from the cosmos. It is one of hundreds of chi kung types available today. Some chi kung types are comparatively simple, with only a few exercises; others can be very extensive, with hundreds of exercises. Shaolin Cosmos Chi Kung belongs to the extensive group. However, chi kung exercises are usually not exclusive to one school, and many of the exercises in Shaolin Cosmos Chi Kung are also found in other types of chi kung.

The exercises in this book form only a part of the repertoire of Shaolin Cosmos Chi Kung. They have been selected because of their excellent benefits for health and vitality. Other Shaolin Cosmos Chi Kung exercises, especially those concerning martial arts and spiritual development, such as Golden Bell, Dragon Strength, Small Universe, Big Universe, and No-Mind Meditation are not described.

The basic chi kung exercises in this book consist of the following:

(A) Ten Shaolin Dynamic Patterns
1 Lifting the Sky (p 22)
2 Plucking Stars (p 24)
3 Pushing Mountains (p 30)
4 Carrying the Moon (p 32)
5 Circulating Head (p 34)
6 Merry-Go-Round (p 36)

7 Big Windmill (p 39)
8 Hula-Hoop (p 41)
9 Deep Knee Bending (p 43)
10 Circulating Knees (p 46)

(B) Self-Manifested Movement (or Induced Chi Flow)

1 Forward-Backward Movement (p 58)
2 Circular Movement (p 61)

(C) Abdominal Breathing (p 76)

(D) Meditation

1 Standing Meditation (p 90)
2 Sitting Meditation (p 92)

There are also the following supplementary exercises:

1 Relaxation exercise to manage stress
2 Circulating Hands to increase internal force
3 Breath co-ordination for better stamina
4 Creative visualization to improve performance
5 Meditation technique to solve problems
6 Meditation technique to enhance creativity

For convenience, training programmes may be classified into two major groups: daily programmes for long-term aims and objectives, and special *ad hoc* programmes for immediate specific needs.

Daily Programmes

The following daily programmes are arranged for a training session of 30 minutes each, once or twice a day for a period of three months.

Programme 1: Complete Sequence

All ten dynamic patterns	10 mins
Self-Manifested Chi Movement	7 mins
Abdominal Breathing	8 mins
Standing Meditation	5 mins

This programme is comprehensive; it covers all the basic exercises presented in this book. It serves as a good introduction to long term holistic chi kung training.

Start by practising all the ten Shaolin dynamic patterns taught in this book. Because only ten minutes are allotted for the ten patterns, you can perform each pattern only a few times. After this, stand still, close your eyes, and proceed to Self-Manifested Chi Movement. The repetition of the ten patterns will serve as the inducing movements. Then gracefully stop your self-manifested movements and proceed to Abdominal Breathing. Complete the session with Standing Meditation.

Programme 2: Dynamic Pattern Selection

Four selected dynamic patterns	10 mins
Self-Manifested Chi Movement	7 mins
Abdominal Breathing	8 mins
Standing Meditation	5 mins

An example of pattern selection:

Session 1	Patterns 1, 2, 3, 4
Session 2	Patterns 3, 4, 5, 6
Session 3	Patterns 5, 6, 7, 8
Session 4	Patterns 7, 8, 9, 10
Session 5	Patterns 9, 10, 1, 2 ... etc

This programme is similar to Programme 1, except that you practise only four dynamic patterns instead of all ten each training session. At the beginners' stage, practising a pattern only a few times may not be sufficient to generate a noticeable effect. Hence, this programme gives you the advantage of spending more time on the respective selected patterns to get better effect, instead of spreading out your effort.

Programme 3: Selection with Constant Emphasis

Four patterns with two constants	15 mins
Abdominal Breathing	7 mins
Standing Meditation	8 mins

An example of pattern selection:

Session 1   Patterns 1, 2, 3, 7
Session 2   Patterns 4, 5, 3, 7
Session 3   Patterns 6, 8, 3, 7
Session 4   Patterns 9, 10, 3, 7
Session 5   Patterns 1, 2, 3, 7 ... etc

Once every four days practise Forward-Backward Movement and Circular Movement instead of Abdominal Breathing and Standing Meditation.

In this programme, one or more dynamic patterns are chosen as constants to be practised every session, to emphasize particular needs or objectives. In this example, Patterns 3 and 7 (Pushing Mountains and Big Windmill) are selected as constants because the student, being a martial artist, wishes to develop internal force in his arms and hands. A student with sexual problems may want to choose Patterns 4 and 8 (Carrying the Moon and Hula-Hoop) as constants.

Self-Manifested Chi Movement is not included in the daily practice. This is to give more time for the development of internal force in the arms and hands. Nevertheless, Self-Manifested Chi Movement is performed regularly once every few days, to cleanse insidious injury as well as maintain practice of the technique.

Programme 4: Selection for Self-Manifested Chi Movement

Three dynamic patterns   8 mins
Self-Manifested Chi Movement   12 mins
Abdominal Breathing   5 mins
Standing Meditation   5 mins

Some good combinations to generate Self-Manifested Chi Movement (or Induced Chi Flow) are as follows:

Patterns 1, 3, 4   for overall flow
Patterns 5, 6, 10   for circular flow
Patterns 3, 4, 7   for flow to arms
Patterns 7, 9, 10   for flow to legs

This programme emphasizes Self-Manifested Chi Movement, and is specially useful for those who wish to practise chi kung for healing general or specific illness. Select three appropriate patterns from the suggested combinations, or choose your own combination, to induce the desired kind of chi flow. A student with rheumatic pain in his legs, for example, may practise the combination of Patterns 7, 9 and 10 more frequently, but he should also try other combinations for variety as well as for balance. After enjoying Self-Manifested Chi Movement, practise Abdominal Breathing to enhance energy levels, and Standing Meditation to still the mind.

Programme 5: Emphasis on Chi Development

One constant and one selected pattern	5 mins
Abdominal Breathing	20 mins
Standing Meditation	5 mins

Dynamic pattern sequence:

Session 1	Patterns 1, 2
Session 2	Patterns 1, 3
Session 3	Patterns 1, 4
Session 4	Patterns 1, 5 ... etc

While Programme 4 emphasizes chi circulation, with its chief aim of harmonious chi flow, this programme emphasizes chi development, with the chief aim of increasing the practitioner's energy level. This programme, therefore, is more suitable for the intermediate level, where the student is comparatively free from illness, and the objectives of training are more inclined towards vitality and internal force. (At the beginners' level, it is better to emphasize the patterns that encourage more chi flow.) When the student is more advanced, he may use Sitting Meditation instead of Standing Meditation; the lotus position is particularly beneficial.

In the preliminary dynamic exercise, Pattern 1, Lifting the Sky, is chosen as a constant because it is an excellent introduction. Of course, other students, for various reasons, may prefer other patterns as constants. Because the main aim here is to develop energy, it is not necessary to perform Self-Manifested Chi Movement. Indeed, you should keep fairly still after practising the dynamic exercises. However, once in a while it is useful to include Self-Manifested Chi Movement in this daily programme.

Programmes for Special Needs

In addition to the daily programmes suggested above, the following are *ad hoc* programmes for immediate needs. They should be performed for about ten minutes each, and once the needs are met the programmes need not be repeated.

Programme 6: Energizing

Merry-Go-Round	5 mins
Simplified Sitting Meditation	5 mins

Suppose you feel tired at your office, but need to meet an important visitor in fifteen minutes. You do not merely want to look fresh, but need to be mentally alert to handle a significant appointment.

Perform the Merry-Go-Round about three times each side. Feel vital energy spreading from your ming men (gate of life) vital point at the centre-back of your waist all over your body. Then perform the Simplified Sitting Meditation for five minutes forgetting about everything and enjoying the tranquillity. You may, if you prefer, just lie comfortably on a couch, instead of sitting upright during meditation. Your visitor will be surprised at how calm and radiant you are.

Programme 7: Nurturing Calmness and Confidence

Abdominal Breathing	5 mins
Standing Meditation	5 mins

If you are supposed to give a talk, demonstration or any public performance, and you feel rather nervous, the above *ad hoc* programme can be helpful in calming you and giving you confidence. Stand upright and relax. Smile from the heart. Then perform Abdominal Breathing for about five minutes. As your manner of breathing has a direct relationship with your temperament, this will make you calm and also provide you with energy. Continue with Standing Meditation for another five minutes, which will make you mentally fresh and alert.

Programme 8: Effective Digestion

Lifting the Sky	2 mins
Big Windmill	5 mins
Circulating Knees	3 mins

If, you have just eaten a sumptuous dinner and you feel drowsy and uncomfortable, or you have to perform some vigorous exercise, and the heavy stomach makes this difficult, you can 'loosen the stomach' and digest the food fast by using this programme. Perform Lifting the Sky a few times to stimulate general chi flow and stretch your body. Then perform Big Windmill, visualizing your chi massaging your stomach to digest the food. Complete with Circulating Knees.

Programme 9: Relieving Pain

Carrying the Moon	5 mins
Self-Manifested Chi Movement	5 mins

If you have back pain, or pain inside your body and medication has not been helpful, the following chi kung exercise is often effective in relieving the pain. Perform Carrying the Moon for five minutes. This will loosen your back muscles as well as engendering energy flow. When your body starts to sway, enjoy the self-manifested chi movements, gently thinking of your vital energy flushing out the pain.

Programme 10: Normalizing Breathing

Lifting the Sky	3 mins
Abdominal Breathing	7 mins

Use these exercises if, after running some distance, playing a vigorous game, or completing some strenuous exercise, you are panting and your heart is beating fast and you wish to return to normal breathing quickly. Perform Lifting the Sky a few times to regulate your breathing and harmonize your chi flow. Then perform Abdominal Breathing, which will make your breathing slow, deep and gentle, and replenish your energy.

18

CAN YOU PLEASE TELL ME?

Some Common Questions and Answers

❖ *A good chi kung book is very useful; it can often*
provide information not found in chi kung classes.

The following are answers to questions students and other people have frequently asked me during my many years of teaching chi kung. They are classified into convenient groups, and arranged according to the level of complexity.

Who Can Practise Chi Kung?

Can children practise chi kung?

Yes, any normal person between seven and seventy can practise chi kung efficiently. Those below seven and above seventy can practise chi kung too, but special attention has to be given, because the younger ones are usually too impatient, and the older ones too slow in their learning.

Can pregnant women practise chi kung?

Yes, but it is often not recommended. Actually, practising chi kung correctly is good for both expectant mothers and their babies. However, there is a risk that should they practise wrongly, the foetus may be harmed. For example, if a pregnant woman stretches her arms upwards too vigorously, as in Lifting the Sky, it may have an adverse effect on the baby. However, if she is competent in chi kung, very gentle chi kung exercise, gentle breathing and meditation are all beneficial. Experience shows that chi kung students who gently visualized in their meditation that they would pleasantly deliver healthy babies, actually did so.

Can a woman practise chi kung during menstruation?

Yes. But if the practice causes an excessive flow, which is unlikely, it is advisable to stop the practice for the time being. For those whose menstruation is not regular, chi kung often helps to regulate it, as chi kung practice brings about hormonal balance.

Can people of different age and sex practise the same type of chi kung?

Generally they can. All the basic chi kung exercises described in this book, for example, are suitable for any normal male or female between seven and seventy. However, the supplementary meditation techniques for problem solving and for creativity are not suitable for children, and not suitable for those who have not attained a 'steady' state of mind. On the other hand, since there is a wide range of chi kung exercises, it is a good idea to choose appropriate exercises for different age and sex groups according to their requirements.

Places of Training

Can we practise chi kung indoors?

We can, but outdoors is preferred, unless the weather is unfavourable or when the type of chi kung, such as meditation or certain techniques involving massage of the sex organs, requires privacy. Taking in cosmic energy (translated as fresh air for simplicity) is an important aspect of chi kung practice. Practising in a congested place, like a closed room, may bring more harm than benefit, because the practitioner is taking in and circulating stale air which may be poisonous to his body cells.

What types of place are good for chi kung practice?

In your garden or a public park, beside a stream or waterfall, on a hill, facing an open sea or open sky.

What types of places should we avoid when practising chi kung?

Crowded and noisy places, where the air is stale or smelly, near a rubbish dump, at or near a cemetery, near factories and heavy traffic.

Times of Training

What is the best time to practise chi kung?

The two best times are at sunrise and at midnight. The hours between seven and nine in the morning, between five and seven in the evening, and between nine and eleven at night are also favourable.

Are there any times that are not suitable for practising chi kung?

Do not practise chi kung at noon, when the weather is very hot, when there is lightning and thunder, when you are on a moving vehicle, or when you are emotionally disturbed.

Food and Hygiene

Can we practise chi kung after a heavy meal?

It is advisable to rest for at least 15 minutes, preferably half an hour, after a heavy meal before practising chi kung. Meditation, however, is permissible after a heavy meal. If your meal is light, you may practise chi kung immediately. It is also not advisable to practise chi kung with an empty stomach. (The chi kung exercises suggested in Programme 9 in Chapter 17 will be helpful to 'loosen' your stomach if you have to participate in vigorous activities after a heavy meal.)

Can we take a bath after or before practising chi kung?

Taking a bath or shower after chi kung practice will keep you fresh, but it is advisable to wait for about 15 minutes before doing so. If you are in a hurry, an acceptable arrangement is to dry your body thoroughly, and walk about briskly but leisurely for at least 50 steps before your bath or shower. After a bath or shower, it is advisable to wait for about five minutes before practising chi kung.

Must a chi kung practitioner abstain from any kinds of food?

No. In fact one remarkable benefit of chi kung is to enable the practitioner to enjoy whatever kinds of food he wishes to eat. Good news for those who love cakes and chocolate as much as their shape!

A chi kung instructor told me it was very important to abstain from food like salted vegetables, radishes and sour fruit. What is your comment?

He must have good reasons to give that advice, and if you practise his type of chi kung, you must follow his advice. But if you practise my type of chi kung, Shaolin Cosmos Chi Kung, it is not necessary to abstain from these types of food, unless, of course, you have other reasons to do so, like being allergic to the food or suffering from an illness that reacts unfavourably to it. Such food actually produces types of energy in the body that hamper smooth energy flow, but a normal person, without chi kung training, can cleanse this negative energy naturally. When you practise chi kung, this cleansing function is enhanced. Therefore, I feel it is unnecessary to restrain students from food which they could readily eat before.

Supplementary Food or Medicine

Is it necessary to supplement chi kung training with tonics or medicine?

No. Chi kung is the best tonic and the best medicine. A Chinese saying goes like this: 'Nourishing with medicine is inferior to nourishing with food; nourishing with food is inferior to nourishing with chi'. Chi kung nourishment or therapy is also the most natural. Chinese medical philosophy explains that when a person takes medicine to cure illness or good food to strengthen himself, the medicine and food produce energy for healing and strengthening. When we take in cosmic energy in chi kung training, the energy heals and strengthens directly, without having to go through the processes of digestion and absorption, producing little or no waste products.

We drink a warm ginger concoction every time we practise chi kung, and it produces a lot of chi. Is this necessary in your type of chi kung?

No. Ginger produces good energy that encourages smooth energy flow. It is sometimes used in Chinese medicine. Nevertheless, in our school of chi kung, we prefer to tap cosmic energy instead.

Mixing Different Types of Chi Kung

I have practised another style of chi kung. Can I mix it with your style?

Yes, and mixing styles will have great advantages as both types of chi kung will benefit each other. Because of your chi kung experience you will progress faster than other students; and when you perform your previous style of chi kung you will attain a higher level than before.

My instructor said that our type of chi kung cannot be mixed with other types. Do you agree?

I disagree. Some special chi kung techniques may clash with other special techniques if their objectives are opposite. For example, some techniques focus energy at the bottom dan tian (energy field) near the sex organs to enhance sexual performance, whereas others focus energy at the top dan tian at the crown of the head for mental or spiritual development. If you practise these different techniques during the same period their effects may cancel each other. These are chi kung techniques, not chi kung types. A chi kung type usually has many techniques. Your chi kung type, in my opinion, does not clash with mine, nor with other types. Perhaps it is because of policy differences, rather than because of the type of chi kung itself, that your instructor asked you not to mix with other types of chi kung.

Dispersing Chi

In my type of chi kung, I have to 'disperse' chi before I complete my practice. I notice that this is not done in your type. Why is there this difference?

Different types of chi kung have different methods of training. Sometimes different instructors teaching the same type of chi kung may use different approaches. If you practise your type of chi kung, you must follow the methods taught by your instructor.

In Shaolin Cosmos Chi Kung, we do not 'disperse' chi. In fact, we aim to develop more chi; dispersing it would be a wastage. As to why you have to disperse chi in your type of chi kung, you must ask your master, for he will be the best person to answer this question. Nevertheless, since so many people have asked me this question, I shall attempt an answer, but I must stress that the answer is my opinion and may not be correct.

In your chi kung you let chi flow at the skin level of your body, which often makes you move or vibrate involuntarily. This has good effect for health, and this seems to be the main aim at this stage. You do not aim to develop chi, nor to control chi flow, which are more advanced stages in your chi kung. Hence, you have to disperse this chi at the completion of your practice otherwise it may flow into your body, and because you do not know how to control it, it may cause serious injury. Dispersing chi, at this stage, is therefore a very good way to prevent possible injury. The disadvantage, however, is that you cannot accumulate chi, and thus cannot progress to advanced stages even if you practise for a long time.

Your master may have mentioned many times that those who wish to proceed to advanced stages must learn from him personally or at least from his selected disciples. You must not misunderstand this as a selfish move. This arrangement is necessary because advanced chi kung, which needs personal supervision to prevent deviation, cannot be taught *en masse* in the same way that chi kung is taught to beginners. There are always pros and cons in everything. Although dispersing chi will limit students to the elementary stage, it cannot be denied that your type of chi kung has brought benefit to a tremendously large number of people, an achievement that may not have been possible if these people had not been given a safeguard against deviation through dispersing chi. Your master, therefore, has a very good reason to ask students at the beginners' level to disperse chi.

Correct Breathing

Is correct breathing important in chi kung?

It is. Wrong breathing in advanced chi kung may cause serious injury.

We practise our chi kung in a big group, with a tape recorder providing background music and instruction on when to breathe in and out. The problem is that after some time our movements may not synchronize with the broadcast instruction, with the result that while following the instruction, we may be breathing in when we should be breathing out. How can we overcome this problem?

I can suggest three ways to overcome this problem. One, breathe naturally, ignoring the instructions if you are not sure. Two, breathe out whenever you stretch, in whenever you withdraw; out whenever you exert, in whenever you relax. Three, follow the instructions throughout, not worrying whether your movements actually synchronize with the broadcast music. Except when practising special techniques where correct breathing is crucial, generally it does not matter very much whether you are breathing in or out at any exact moment as long as you are rhythmic in your breathing. Usually when chi kung is practised publicly in big groups, the level of chi aimed at is not very high; advanced chi kung needs personal supervision. (This does not mean group chi kung is not good. Indeed chi kung practised *en masse* has benefited many people.) Hence, even if you have made mistakes in your breathing, the side-effects will be slight, and can usually be remedied in the process of your chi kung practice.

Tai Chi Chuan (Taijiquan)

Is chi kung the same as Tai Chi Chuan (Taijiquan)?

They are different. Basically, Tai Chi Chuan is a martial art, though most people nowadays practise it exclusively for health. Chi kung is basically for health, though many people apply it for martial arts, mental performance and spiritual development. If you want to attain advanced levels in Tai Chi Chuan, whether for fighting or for health, you have to practise chi kung, because without proper chi training it is impossible to develop the internal force which gives Tai Chi Chuan its combative excellence as well as its health benefits.

Sex

Must one abstain from sex to practise chi kung?

No. In fact, for both men and women, practising chi kung will enhance one's performance and enjoyment of sex; but one must not use this bonus licentiously.

Does having sex affect a person's level of chi?

Yes. For this reason, in the past serious chi kung students abstained from sex for the first 100 days of their chi kung training, so as to build a pearl of energy as foundation for subsequent practice. After this period they carried on their normal sex life. In the past, practising chi kung was a rare opportunity, so many students were prepared to make this initial sacrifice. But nowadays, I feel this sacrifice is not necessary, because not only is chi kung readily available now, but also students do not have such high expectations of their attainments in chi kung as they did in the past. Having sex during the first 100 days will certainly slow down progress, but modern needs are such that it is more practical for most people to carry on their normal sex lives and achieve the chi foundation in 200 or even 300 days, than to abstain and achieve it in 100 days.

Can we have sex immediately after chi kung practice?

Please don't, for that will drain away a lot of chi. It is advisable to wait for an hour, or at least half an hour if you can't wait that long. On the other hand, performing chi kung after sex is recommended, as that will help to replenish energy.

Keeping the Mind Still

I find it very hard to keep the mind still or empty. Can you give me some advice?

All untrained people find it hard to keep the mind still or empty. Hence the Chinese refer to the constant thoughts of the untrained mind as monkeys and wild horses. But the mind can be kept still, and many people have done it. A very useful principle is 'Let one thought replace a hundred thoughts'. It is difficult to still hundreds of thoughts that arise in the mind; but it is not so difficult to focus the mind on one thought. When we succeed in keeping the mind on only one thought, that is the same as keeping the mind free from all other thoughts. Then we can even keep out this one thought, thus achieving an empty mind. This one thought can be a constant object, like a stone or your abdomen; a prayer or a nonsensical verse; counting your breaths in sets of ten or mindfully following your chi kung movements. One concluding piece of advice: you have to put in time and effort to practise this principle before you can be competent.

Learning from a Book

Can we learn chi kung from a book?

To answer this question thoroughly, we have to consider three factors: the reader, the book, and the kind of chi kung.

If the reader is well versed in chi kung, he will benefit much from reading a good chi kung book. He will have no difficulty performing the exercises described in the book. A beginner will have much difficulty. Even if he can understand the text, he may not be able to practise the exercises correctly.

If the book is full of philosophical concepts literally translated from Chinese, it may be difficult for readers to understand. For example, expressions like 'water chi combines with fire chi to produce real chi', which is concise to the initiated, is meaningless to most readers. But if the book is well written, with the readers' easy comprehension in mind, the readers can not only derive much information, but also follow the exercises that are systematically described and illustrated. The above expression becomes meaningful if written as 'energy from the kidneys reacts with energy from the heart to produce vital energy that sustains life'.

Chi kung knowledge can be readily conveyed in a good book, but chi kung techniques, even clearly explained, may not be correctly followed by readers with no chi kung experience. Even a simple movement like lifting a hand in a particular manner, for example, cannot be easily described in words. Therefore, for complete beginners it is advisable to learn from an instructor. However, a good chi kung book is very useful; it can often provide information not normally found in formal chi kung classes.

NOTES

Chapter 1: Treat Yourself to the Secrets of the Ancient Masters

1 Lin Hou Sheng and Lok Pei Yi, *Three Hundred Questions on Qigong*, Guangdong Science and Technology Publishing House, 1983, p 38–42. In Chinese.
2 Li Shou Kang, *Qigong Therapy and Health*, Te Li Books, Hong Kong, 1974, p 17. In Chinese.
3 Ibid, p 24
4 Ibid, p 27–8

Chapter 9: Take a Drink of Cosmic Energy

1 McAleer, Neil, *The Cosmic Mind-Boggling Book*, Warner Books, New York, 1982, p xii

Chapter 10: Tranquillity of Joy and Inner Peace

1 Lao Tzu, *Tao Te Ching*, [The Classic of Taoism], Chapter 25. Taken from the ancient text for free distribution by Divine Heaven Society, Taiwan. In Chinese.
2 Hui Neng, *The Platform Sutra*, Section 53. In Chinese.
3 *The Upanishads*, selected and translated by Swami Prabhavananda and Frederick Manchester, Mentor Books, New York, 1975, p 13
4 James, William, *The Varieties of Religious Experience*, Mentor Books, New York, 1958, p 313
5 Cited in: Najib Ullah, *Islamic Literature*, Washington Square Press Inc, New York, 1963, p 159
6 Quoted in: Valiuddin, Dr Mir, *Contemplative Disciplines in Sufism*, East-West Publications, London, 1980, p 160
7 K. Sri Dhammananda, *Meditation: The Only Way*, Buddhist Missionary

Society, Kuala Lumpur, 1987, p 33
8 Scott Rogo, D, *Our Psychic Potentials*, Prentice Hall Press, New York, 1984, p 83

Chapter 12: Meet the Masters and Know Their Arts

1 *Introduction to Waitankung*, China's Television Company, Taipei, Taiwan, 1981. In Chinese. (This booklet is a report of the Taiwanese television interview with Sifu Zhang and the subsequent daily broadcasts of his Waitankung exercises in 1980.)
2 This means 'energy that is already in us'.
3 This refers to the pearl of energy accumulated at the abdominal energy field.
4 This is typical Taoist chi kung terminology. It means that improved circulation of blood and other fluids enhances our physical body. (Fluid generates essence.) An improved physical body enhances health and vitality. (Essence generates energy.) Better health and vitality promotes mental and spiritual growth. (Energy generates spirit.)
5 They refer to the following energy fields: baihui (at the crown of the head), qihai (3in. below the navel) and huiying (near the anus). In Chinese, energy fields are called dan tian.
6 In the original text, Sifu Zhang gave the Taoist terms for these 'palaces', such as 'danyuan palace of the kidneys', 'zhuling palace of the intestines', 'lantai palace of the liver' etc. To avoid confusion, these terms are left out in the translation; this does not affect the meaning of the passage. In Taoist philosophy the 'palace' is where the spirit of the organ is located.
7 *Introduction to Waitankung*, p 6
8 Li Zhi Yong, *History of Chinese Qigong*, Science and Technology Publications, Henan, 1988, p 423. In Chinese.
9 Ibid, p 425
10 In Western terms, this may be translated as 'If a person is physically (essence), physiologically (energy) and psychologically (spirit) fit, he is healthy'.
11 Lin Hou Sheng and Gu Qun, *Taiji Qigong Eighteen Steps*, Chinese Medical and Pharmacological College Publishing House, Shanghai, 1987, pp 2–5
12 Ibid, pp 9–11
13 An inner-chamber disciple is a special disciple to whom the master passes on advanced, often secret, aspects of the art.
14 In advanced chi kung, a master may, for example, transmit chi impulses into water for a patient to drink or onto clothing for a patient to wear, to cure illness or for other beneficial purposes. An analogy from modern science is the transmission of electronic impulses into a diskette so that

audio or visual recordings can be reproduced.

15 If these terms sound odd, it is because of the cultural and linguistic differences between Chinese and English. In the Chinese language the terms are meaningful as well as poetic.

16 In Chinese medical philosophy the kidney is responsible for vitality, especially sexual vitality.

17 Personal letter from Sifu Chin Chee Ching, 1993

18 Ou Bao Xiang, edited by Chin Chee Ching, *Damo Qigong Therapy and Health*, [Damo Qigong training manual], p 18. In Chinese.

19 Sifu Yap means that the patient moves 'involuntarily' as the result of his enhanced internal chi flow – like the self-manifested movements in induced chi flow.

20 This is similar to Sifu Ou Bao Xiang's demonstration described above.

21 Personal letter from Sifu Yap Soon Yeong, dated 18 March 1993

Chapter 14: Say Goodbye to Stress

1 Restak, Richard, MD, *The Brain*, Bantam Books, Toronto, 1984, p 184.

2 Dong Jiang Hua, and Ma Ming Ren, *Practical Chinese Psychology*, Beijing Publishing House, 1987, pp 127–8. In Chinese.

3 Ibid, pp 127–172

4 Cited in Zhou Chang Fa (*et al*), *Stories of Psychiatric Treatment in Ancient China*, Jiangsu Science and Technology Publications, 1987, pp 42–4. In Chinese.

5 Ibid, pp 53–4

6 Wang Ji Sheng, *Psychology of Chinese Qigong*, China's Social Science Publishing House, 1989, p 6. In Chinese.

7 Ibid, pp 14–15

8 Ibid, pp 16–24

Chapter 15: Energy and Stamina for Champions

1 Xie Huan Zhang, *Scientific Basis for Qigong*, University of Science and Technology Publications, Beijing, 1988, p 242. In Chinese.

2 Bei Jia Te *et al*, 'Application of Qigong to Promote Standards of Sports', in Qigong Magazine, Vol. 3, No. 1, Jijiang Science and Technology Publications, 1982, p.32. In Chinese.

3 Ibid, pp 32–3

4 Xie Huan Zhang, *Scientific Basis of Qigong*, p 247

5 Ibid, p 241

Chapter 16: Reaching for the Remarkable and the Divine

1   Mystical Experiences of Medieval Saints. Quoted in: Johnson, Julian, *The Path of the Masters*, Radha Soami Satsang Beas, Punjab, 1988, p 332
2   Ephesians 4:6
3   Valiuddin, Dr Mir, *Contemplative Disciplines in Sufism*, East-West Publications, London, 1980, p 114
4   Ibid, p 115

GLOSSARY

Abdominal Breathing   A chi kung breathing technique whereby the practitioner takes in cosmic energy and stores it at his **abdominal energy field.**

abdominal energy field   A chi kung term referring to a space about two or three inches below the navel where a practitioner focuses his vital energy. *See also* 'dan tian'.

alaya consciousness   A Buddhist term referring to the collective consciousness of a class of beings, which has been formulated throughout the millennia, and which affects the way that class of beings perceive reality. For example, because humans and bacteria have different alaya consciousness, a human and a bacterium will perceive the same phenomenon differently.

baihui   A **vital point** at the crown of the head. **Baihui** in Chinese literally means 'the meeting of hundred meridians'.

Big Universe   An advance chi kung exercise whereby **vital energy** is made to flow through all the twelve **primary meridians** in the body, namely the meridians of the lung, colon, stomach, spleen, heart, intestine, bladder, kidney, pericardium, triple warmer, gall bladder and liver. It is also known as the Macrocosmic Flow.

Chan Buddhism   Chinese term for **Zen Buddhism,** the school of Buddhism initiated by Bodhidharma at the Shaolin Monastery and later spread to Vietnam, Korea, Japan and other parts of the world.

chi kung state of mind   A heightened (or deepened) mental state in chi kung practice whereby the practitioner is not bothered about external stimuli. It is similar to the alpha level of mind in Western terminology. In classical chi kung terms it is known as 'ru jing' or 'enter silence'.

cosmic energy   Energy existing freely in the cosmos, and is known as 'tian chi' in Chinese,. It is more than just air.

dan tian   A chi kung term in Chinese meaning elixir field or energy field. It is a space in his body where a practitioner focuses and accumulates his vital energy. There can be many **dan tians** in the body, such as at the crown of the head, the solar plexis and the centre of the palms, but if the term is used in an unqualified way it usually refers to the **abdominal energy field,**

dynamic chi kung   A genre of chi kung exercises where bodily movements are obvious, as distinguished from **quiescent chi kung** where the practitioner remains in a relatively stationary position.

energy field   *Please see* **dan tian.**

energy point   *Please see* **vital point.**

five elemental processes   A fundamental Chinese philosophical concept, known as 'wu xing', which advocates that the myriad processes in the universe may be classified into five archetypes symbolized by the processes of metal, water, wood, fire and earth. It is usually misinterpreted as five elements.

Han Dynasty   207 BCE to 220 CE. This was the golden age of Chinese science. China consists of many races and languages; what is generally referred to as the Chinese race is actually the Han race, as distinct from other minority races in China like the Manchurians and the Tibetans; what is generally referred to as the Chinese language is the Han language.

hard chi kung   Martial art chi kung where internal force and sometimes external hard conditioning are often used in its training. Examples include Golden Bell, Iron Shirt and Iron Palm.

heart   In Chinese the term **heart** often refers to what Westerners would call 'mind'.

huiyin   A **vital point** situated between the sex organ and the anus. **Huiyin** in Chinese literally means 'meeting of two yins'.

inner-chamber disciple   Disciple specially selected by a master for advanced, often secret, training.

meditation   A training of the mind to reach different levels of consciousness. It also refers to a genre of chi kung exercises which emphasizes this training.

meridian   Pathway of energy flow in the body, known as 'mai' in Chinese. There are two sets of meridians: the twelve primary meridians which flow through the internal organs, namely the meridians of the lung, colon, stomach, spleen, heart, intestine, bladder, kidney, pericardium, triple warmer, gall bladder and liver; and the eight secondary or wondrous meridians which do not flow through any organs, namely ren mai, du mai, chong mai, dai mai, yin qiao, yang qiao, yin wei and yang weo.

ming men   A vital point at the back of the body opposite the navel. In Chinese **ming men** literally means 'the gate of life'.

muraqaba   A Muslim term referring to a heightened, or deepened, state of mind where the devotee attains a union with God.

naohu   A vital point at the back of the head where the spine enters the skull. In Chinese **naohu** means 'the house of the brain'.

orison   A Christian term referring to a heightened, or deepened, state of mind whereby the devotee experiences God.

qigong   The Romanized Chinese spelling for 'chi kung'. The pronunciation of 'qigong' and 'chi kung' is the same.

quiescent chi kung   A genre of chi kung exercises where there is little or no external movements, as the emphasis is on internal energy flow and visualization. *See also* **dynamic chi kung.**

self-induced chi flow   *Please see* **self-manifested chi movement.**

self-manifested chi movement   A genre of chi kung exercises whereby the practitioner may move about without his volution. It is also called **self-induced chi flow.**

Shaolin Kungfu   The most widely practised form of kung fu in the world today. It was initially developed in the Shaolin Monastery in China, and branched into numerous styles.

Sifu   A Chinese term meaning 'master'. **Sifu** is the Cantonese pronunciation, in standard Chinese (or Mandarin), it is pronounced as 'shifu'.

Sitting Meditation   A meditation exercise whereby the practitioner sits crossed legged in a lotus position, or upright on a seat while meditating.

Small Universe   An advanced chi kung exercise whereby energy is made to flow continuously round the body through the ren mai and the du mai. It is also called the Microcosmic Flow.

Song Dynasty   Pronounced and also spelt as Sung Dynasty, 960 to 1279 BCE, when the Chinese arts of silk making, jade carving and ceramics reached their heights.

Standing Meditation A meditation exercise whereby the practitioner stands upright while meditating.

Tai Chi Chuan *Please see* **Taijiquan.**

Taiji Eighteen Steps Chi Kung A modern form of chi kung developed in mainland China and is popularly practised outside China. It is not the same as **Taijiquan** (Tai Chi Chuan) or Taiji Chi Kung.

Taijiquan A major form of kung fu which emphasizes internal training or chi or energy. Most people today, however, practise Taijiquan for health purposes, often neglecting its combative aspect. It is also spelt as Tai Chi Chuan.

Tang Dynasty 618 to 906, The golden age of Chinese art and culture. Today many Chinese, especially overseas Chinese, refer to themselves as the Tang people, and to the Chinese (or Han) language as the Tang language.

Universal Mind *Please see* **Yi Xin.**

vital energy The energy inside our body responsible for keeping us alive. It is called 'zhen chi' in Chinese.

vital point Point on the surface of the body where vital energy inside the body may be accessed. It is also called energy point or acu point.

void A Buddhist and a Taoist term referring to the Supreme Reality or Ultimate Truth which is undifferentiated, beyond dualism, and devoid of phenomena.

Waitankung A form of chi kung first developed in Taiwan and is popular outside mainland China.

Yi Xin A Buddhist term in Chinese meaning 'One Mind' or 'Universal Mind'. 'One', here refers to 'one and only'; it means the ultimate reality, or what some people would call God.

yin yang A fundamental Chinese philosophical concept which stipulates that every object, process or idea in the universe has two opposing yet complementary aspects symbolized as yin and yang.

Zen Buddhism A major school of Buddhism that advocates attaining enlightenment in an instant. Its principal approach is meditation. *See also* **Chan Buddhism.**

Zhou Dynasty Also spelt as Chou Dynasty, 1030 to 480 BCE, and known as the classical age of China, during which period the major schools of Chinese philosophy like Taoism and Confucianism were established.

FURTHER READING

In English

Anderson, Watt, *Open Secrets: A Western Guide To Tibetan Buddhism*, Viking Press, New York, 1979

Bahm, Archie, J *Yoga Sutra of Paranjali*, Arnold Heinemann Publishers, New Delhi, 1978

Blofeld, John, *Taoism: the Quest for Immortality*, Unwin Paperbacks, London, 1979

Capra, Fritjof, *The Tao of Physics*, Bantam Books, Toronto, 1984.

Davidson John, *Sutle Energy*, C W Daniel Company, Saffron Walden, 1987

Dharmmananda, K Sri, *Meditation: The Only Way*, Buddhist Missionary Society, Kuala Lumpar, 1987

Dupra, Louis, *The Deeper Life: An Introduction tio Christian Mysticism*, Crossroad Publishing Company, New York, 1981

Eliade, Mircea, *Shamanism, Archaic Techniques of Ecstasy*, translated by Willard R Trask, Arkana, London, 1989

Goleman, Daniel, *The Meditative Mind: The Varieties of Meditative Experience*, Jeremy Tarcher, Los Angeles, 1988

Idries Shah, *The Way of the Sufi*, E P Dutton, New York, 1970

Inglis, Brian, *Science and Parascience*, Hodder and Stoughton, London, 1986

Jacka, Judy, *Frontiers of Natural Therapies*, Lotian Publishing Company, Melbourne, 1989,

James, William, *The Varieties of Religious Experience*, Mentor Books, New York, 1958

Johnson, Julian, *The Path of the Master*, Radha Soami Satsand Beas, Punjab, 1988

Kenyon, Julian N, *Twenty-First Century Medicine*, Thorsons, Wellingborough, 1986

LeShan, Lawrence, *Clairvoyant Reality*, Turnstone Press, Wellingborough, 1982

McLeer, Neil, *The Cosmic Mind-Boggling Book*, Warner Books, New York, 1982

Najib Ullar, Islamic Literature, Washington Square Press Inc, New York, 1963

Morris Richard, *The Nature of Reality*, McGraw Hill, New York, 1987

Palmer, Martin, *The Elements of Taoism*, Element Books, Shaftesbury, 1991

Playfair, Guy Lyion, *Medicine, Mind and Magic*, Aquarian Press, Wellingborough, 1987

Restak, Richard, MD, *The Brain*, Bantam Books, Toronto, 1984

Roussea, Pierre, *The Limits of Science*, translation edited by John Newell, Scientific Book Club, London, 1967

Rogo, D Scott, *Our Psychic Potentials*, Prentice Hall Press, New York, 1984

The Upanishads, selected and translated by Swami Prahavanda and Frederick Manchester, Mentor Books, New York, 1975

Sivananda, Swami, *The Science of Pranayama*, Divine Life Society, Tehri-Garhwal, Himalayas, 1987

Valiuddin, Dr Mir, *Comtemplative Disciplines in Sufism*, East-West Publications, London, 1980

Watson, Lyall, *Beyond Supernature: A New Natural History of the Supernatural*. Hodder and Stoughton, London, 1986

Weed, Joseph J, *How You Can Predict the Future*, Thomas & Co, Wellingborough, 1978

Wong Kiew Kit, Introduction to Saolin Kungfu, Paul Crompton, London, 1981, reprinted 1994

Wong Kiew Kit, *The Art of Chi Kung*, Element Books, Shaftesbury, 1993

Wong Kiew Kit, *The Art of Shaolin Kungfu*, Element Books, Shaftesbury, 1966

Wong Kiew Kit, *The Complete Book of Tai Chi Chuan*, Element Books, Shaftesbury, 1996

Yogananda, Paramahansa, *Autobiography of a Yogi*, Jacio Publishing House, Bombay, 1985

Zukav, Gary, *The Dancing Wu Li Masters: An Overview of the New Physics*, Bantam Books, New York, 1989

In Chinese

Bei Jia Te and others, 'Application of Qigong to Promote Standards of Sports' in *Qigong Magazine*, Vol 3, No 1, Jijiang Science and Technology Publications, 1982

Bha Vana, *Practical Buddhist Meditation for Beginners*, Syarikat Dharma, Kuala Lumpur, 1981

Cheng Yi Shan, *Ancient Chinese Thinking on Qi*, Hupei People's Publications, 1986

Chunwoji Juren, *Secrets of Shaolin Kungfu*, Taiping Books, Hong Kong, 1983

Dong Jiang Hua and Ma Ming Ren, *Practical Chinese Psychology*, Beijing Publishing House, Beijing, 1987

Hu Hai Chang and others (eds), *Collection of Chi Kung Scientific Reports*. University of Science and Technology Publishing House, Beijing, 1989

Hui Neng, *The Platform Sutra*, ancient text

Introduction to Waitankung. Chinas Telivision Company, Taipei, 1981

Lao Tzu, *Tao Te Ching*, ancient text reprinted for free distribution by Divine Heaven Society, Taiwan, undated

Lian Yang the Recluse, *Taoist Immortality and Zen Meditation*, Wuling Publishing House, Taipei, 1988

Liu Zhi Xue (ed), *Collections of Shaolin Material*, Literary and Cultural Publications, Beijing, 1982

Li Wen Tao, *Introduction to Yaiji Chi King*, Guang Qing Publishing House, Kowloon, 1986

Li Ying Ang, *Pictorial Explanation on Shaolin Principles*, reprinted from ancient text, Unicorn Press, Hong Kong, 1968

Li Zhi Yong, *History of Chinese Qigong*, Science and Technology Publications, Henan, 1988

Li Shou Kang, *Qigong Therapy and Health*, Te Li Books, Hong Kong, 1974

Lin Hou Sheng and Gu Qun, *Taiji Qigong Eighteen Steps*, Chinese Medical and Pharmacological College Publishing House, Shanghai, 1987

Lin Hou Sheng and Lok Pei Yi, *Three Hundred Questions on Qigong*, Guandong Science and Technology Publishing House, Guangzhou, 1962

Liu Hua Yang, *The Principles of Meditation in the Attainment of Sainthood*, an ancient text edited by Lian Yang the Recluse, Sunny Books, Taipei, 1988

Ou Bao Xiang and Chin Chee Ching, *Damo Qigong Therapy and Health*, Training, Manual of Damo Qigong, Singapore, 1992

Pei Xi Yong, (ed), *Discourse on Wudang Chi Kung*, Sanlian Books, Shanghai, 1989

Qui Ling, (ed), *Selection of Ancient Chinese Chi Kung*, Guangdon Science and Technology Publications, Guangzhou, 1988

Tao Bing Fu and Yang Wei He (eds), *Fine Collections of Chi Kung Therapeutic Techniques*, People's Health Publishing House, Beijing, 1980

Venerable Sheng Yan, *Experience of Zen, Dafeng Cultural Publications, Taipei, undated*

Wang Ji Sheng, *Psychology of Chinese Qugong*, Chinas Social Science Publishing House, 1989

Xie Huan Zhang, *Scientific Basis for Qigong*, University of Science and Technology Publications, Beijing, 1988

Xu Jing and others, *The Four Great Chi Kung Classics of China*, Jijiang Classical Books Publishers, 1988

Zhang San Feng, *The Secret of Training the Internal Elixir in the Taiji Art*, preserved by TaiyiShanren, reprinted from ancient text by Anhua Publications, Hong Kong, undated

Zhou Chang Fa and others, *Stories of Psychiatric Treatment in Ancient China*, Jiangsu Science and Technology Publications, 1987

USEFUL ADDRESSES

Australia

Master Selina Griffin
Shaolin Wahnam Chi Kung and Taijiquan
RSD Strathfieldsaye Road
Strathfieldsaye, Bendigo
Victoria 3551, Australia
Tel (61–54) 393257

Master John Trevor
Shaolin Wahnam Chi Kung and Taijiquan
PO Box 2088
Murraybridge, SA 5253
Australia
Tel (61–8) 298 8659; (61–85) 321940

Europe

Master Douglas Wiesenthal
Shaolin Wahnam Chi Kung and Kungfu
Crta de Humera, 87, 3–B
Pozeulo de Alarcon
28224 Madrid, Spain.
Tel (34–1) 351 2115
Fax (34–1) 351 2163

Master Rafael Julian Palangues
Shaolin Wahnam Chi Kung and Kungfu
Aptos Media Luna 4–2
12120 Lucena
Spain
Tel (34–64) 380200
Tel (34–64) 245153

Dr Riccardo Salvatore
Shaolin Wahnam Chi Kung and Kungfu
PC Affranio Peixoto 2–101
1000 Lisbon, Portugal
Tel (351–1) 847 8713
Fax (351–1) 847 8713

Master Reimer Buerkner
Shaolin Wahnam Chi Kung
Eichendorff strasse 23
Dreieich, Germany
Tel (49–6103) 84451
Fax (49–6103) 66919

Master Thomas Milanovski
Dragon Chan Qi Dao Kungfu School
Linnestr 6, 60385 Frankfurt
Germany
Tel (49–69) 434389
Fax (49–69) 700891

Master Kai Uwe Jettkandt
Budokan
Burgstrasse 47, 60389 Frankfurt
Germany
Tel (49–69) 453655
Fax (49–69) 768 2104

Master Hugo Bonham
Shaolin Wahnam Chi Kung and Kungfu
Ulmenstr 19, 82256 Fuestenfeldbruck
Germany
Tel (49–8141) 351518
Fax (49–8141) 351594

Master Robert Burkhandt
Shaolin Wahnam Chi Kung and Kungfu
Lessingstr 49, 85646, Anzing
Germany
Tel (49–8121) 1646
Fax (49–8121) 49615

Master Sylvester Lohninger
Shaolin Wahnam Chi Kung
Rimi Dharma Dzong Tierra
Gutenstein, Austria
Tel (43–2634) 4174
Fax (43–2634) 4174

British Tai Chi Chuan and Shaolin Kungfu Association
29 Linden Farm Drive
Countesthorpe
Leicester, LE8 3SX
United Kingdom

Tai Chi Chuan Union of Great Britain
69 Kilpatrick Gardens
Clarkston
Glasgow G76 7RF
Great Britain
Tel (44–374) 985411; (44–141) 6382946

Shaolin Temple Kungfu Association
PO Box 9920
3506 GX Utrecht
Holland
Tel (31–30) 2624400
Fax (31–30) 2620994

Malaysia and Singapore

Master Wong Kiew Kit
Shaolin Wahnam Chi Kung and Kungfu
81 Taman Intan B/5
08000 Sungai Petani, Kedah
Malaysia
Tel (60–4) 422 2353
Fax (60–4) 422 7812

Master Chan Chee Kong
Shaolin Wahnam Chi Kung and Kungfu
301 Block A, Menara Megah
Jalan Kolam Air, Off Jalan Ipoh
Kuala Lumpur, Malaysia
Tel (60–3) 444 2150; 010 211 6036

Master Ng Kowi Beng
Shaolin Wahnam Chi Kung and Kungfu
H & P Plastic Pte Ltd
Plot 935 Lorong Makmur 13/1
Taman Makmur, Mk. Sg Seluang
Daerah Kulim, Malaysia
Tel (60–4) 484 1159
Fax (60–4) 484 1125

Master Goh Kok Hin
Shaolin Wahnam Chi Kung and Kungfu
86 Jalan Sungai Emas
08500 Kota Kuala Muda, Kedah
Malaysia
Tel (60–4) 437 4301

Master Cheong Huat Seng
Shaolin Wahnam Chi Kung and Kungfu
22 Taman Mutiara
08000 Sungai Petani, Kedah
Malaysia
Tel (60–4) 421 0634

Master Yong Peng Wah
Shaolin Wahnam Chi Kung
181 Taman Kota Jaya
34700 Simpang, Taiping
Perak, Malaysia
Tel (60–5) 847 1431

Master Yap Soon Yeong
Yap Qigong Therapy
1–B, Jalan Fetes
11200 Tanjung Bunga
Penang, Malaysia
Tel (60–4) 899 6728

Master Chin Chee Ching
Shaolin Damo Chi Kung
Block 929, 13–477 Tamping St 91
Singapore 520929
Tel (65) 782 9958
Fax (65) 787 3969

USA

Master Richard Mooney
Sarasota Shaolin Academy
4655 Flatbush Avenue
Sarasota, FL 34233–1920
USA

Dr Paul Hannah, MD
Tai Chi Chuan, Baqua and Xingyiquan
2200 Grant Street, Suite 109
Gary, IN 46404, USA
Tel (1–219) 944 9300
Fax (1–219) 944 8735

INDEX